It's a great honor for me to endorse *1 and 2 Thessalonians on F.I.R.E.,* the latest book by Dr. Ken J. Burge, Sr. in the F.I.R.E. series, representing his masterful expository work on the two Pauline epistles to the Thessalonians. As Paul's epistles, 1 and 2 Thessalonians convey important topics with vast instruction. One overarching subject is the certain and impending Rapture and Second Coming of the Lord Jesus Christ. Along with this subject is the "wake-up call" instruction on how Christians should conduct their lives in view of the imminent return of Jesus. Important as these two epistles of Paul are, there is a need of a gifted pastor-teacher to properly expound every verse in each chapter. Fortunately, this need is met in the person of Pastor Burge, Sr. in this work. In *1 and 2 Thessalonians on F.I.R.E.,* we get exactly what we need. This book is helpful both for pastors and laymen.

Pastor Eleordo Gantalao
Pastor Emeritus, Anislag Christian Fellowship,
Calbayog City, Philippines; pastoral staff,
New Hope Community Church, Temecula, CA

Dr. Burge has written a book that is easy to read and has good illustrations; however, there is nothing shallow about this work. If you are looking for scholarly interpretation along with practical application, then *1 and 2 Thessalonians* is the book for you!

Dr. Leandro Tarractaca
President, Abacar Bible College; pastor,
and host of the daily radio show "Truth of the Bible"

This is a brilliant, inductive commentary by Dr. Ken J. Burge, Sr. on the biblical books of 1 and 2 Thessalonians. Unlike most commentaries, Dr. Burge's commentary not only explains the Scripture but also engages the reader as an active participant and guides you to do your own inductive work so you can uncover what the Scripture says for yourself. Furthermore, of all the systematic methods of Bible study that I have seen, the F.I.R.E. method is the most effective and comprehensive; it is both scholarly and devotional—a rare combination indeed. As you read this commentary using the author's four-step method called F.I.R.E., you will become intimately familiar with 1 and 2 Thessalonians and learn how to apply God's Word in your life.

Darius Ward,
Colmar Manor Bible Church;
high-school biology teacher

1 AND 2 THESSALONIANS ON

FAMILIARITY
INTERPRETATION
RELATIONSHIP &
EMPLOYMENT

Dr. Ken J. Burge, Sr.

Deep River BOOKS

1 and 2 Thessalonians on F.I.R.E.

ISBN – 13: 9781632695499
Library of Congress Control Number: 2020912745

Printed in the USA
2020—First Edition
29 28 27 26 25 24 23 22 21 20   10 9 8 7 6 5 4 3 2 1

Cover design by Joe Bailen, Contagus Design

Dedication

My dear wife Kimberly teaches a Bible study class on Sunday mornings for children three to seven years old. Kylee, my eldest grandchild (age six) attends the class weekly. She kept hearing her grandmother say to the class, "Let your light shine for Jesus." Precious Kylee Joy asked, "What does it mean to let your light shine?" Spontaneously, and I believe Spirit-led, Kimberly replied, "You know how Anna shines for the Lord and is always telling people about Jesus. Shining your light means being like Anna, who each day lives for Jesus."

The Lord brought Anna Sanchez Hernandez here from Guatemala. Kimberly and I met her at a diner where she serves as a waitress. God was drawing the heart of this twenty-seven-year-old to Himself; she began a quest to know love and the God of love. Anna later shared with Kimberly and me that she perceived something special in our lives, so she began regularly talking to us and probing for truth.

Subsequently Anna started attending our church, which stretched the limited English vocabulary she possessed. Amazingly her English rapidly developed and she called me on September 25, 2018. This day became memorable for both of us, because Anna placed her faith in the finished work of Jesus. Then on June 23, 2019, I baptized two special young ladies: Kylee Joy and Anna Sanchez. Kylee Joy exhibits the same light that Anna possesses—or rather, that possesses her. Both have a Central American connection, because Kylee's other grandmother (*abuelita*) comes from Nicaragua. With great pleasure I dedicate *1 and 2 Thessalonians on F.I.R.E.* to Kylee Joy Burge and Anna Sanchez Hernandez. May their light for Jesus inspire many to follow the light of the world!

CONTENTS

Requirements for the Future

Continuing Despite Persecution

Clarifying the Day of Christ

Closing Exhortations to the Saints

FOREWORD

Like every gift given to us from God, our Heavenly Father has given the church many gifted leaders, because He loves the church. In Ephesians 4:11–12, the apostle Paul wrote to the church that Christ gave "pastors and teachers, for the equipping of the saints," with the result that the children of God should not be tossed about by the winds of false doctrine that blow through the church, wreaking havoc among the flock. Along with building a shelter from false doctrine, the pastors and teachers of the church are to open the eyes of the saints to the satanic trickery, craftiness, and deceitful schemes of the enemy (Eph. 4:14).

How has the Lord ordained this safeguarding of the soul to happen in His church? Through the ordinary means of the proclamation and teaching of the Word of God. By the preaching and teaching of the Bible the people of God are exposed to the mind of Christ and given a profound view of God Himself. They see how they should live in the world and behave in the church. They are given many precious promises that act like anchors in the storms of life. The teaching of Scripture has been the duty of every faithful shepherd in the church since the time of the apostles. Where spiritual weakness and immaturity exists, and where carnal living and sin abound, you can be sure that either the Word is not being taught or the people are not heeding its warnings.

The book you hold in your hands shows that Pastor Ken Burge takes seriously the charge to equip the saints for the work of the ministry. Probably going back to the Middle Ages, the church has been divided in a way that God never intended. Biblical scholars and theological academics have holed themselves up in the lofty towers of higher education and have for the most part segregated themselves from the practical matters within the church and the world. And to make matters worse, most of those who choose to serve the church as pastors, missionaries, and spiritual leaders have taken up practical theology and the application of the Word as their duty while leaving the weightier matters for the academics to wrestle with, sometimes coming to the false conclusion that deep thinking and doctrine do not belong in the pulpit or the church.

Dr. Burge is a churchman of the best kind. He is a pastor-scholar who cares for the church and the Word. His desire is to lead people to know the Scriptures so that they can know the God of the Scriptures. In his study of Paul's Thessalonian epistles, he has gone verse by verse, and often word by word, through these important books of the New Testament to mine the riches of the text. You will find frequent word studies, and even grammatical analyses referencing the Greek New Testament. But as a scholar with a shepherd's heart, he has not forgotten that theology is the handmaiden to the church. With his F.I.R.E. system, Pastor Burge teaches his reader how to "do" Bible study in a way that will stretch the average Christian, but without frustrating the reader with minutiae and overly technical language. As Pastor Burge explains a verb tense, he shows why this insight is important for understanding the passage. He demonstrates that the cultural background is key to getting into the sandals of the apostle Paul and his readers, and shows what the text means before jumping to application too quickly.

When "employment" or application is given, we again see the pastor's heart come out in Ken. As I read his words, I could immediately sense that he cares for the reader as he does his own flock. He is not simply interested in transferring information (although he is), but desires to see hearts set aflame for the glory of God and for the joy of the child of God. In short, he wants what every genuine pastor wants—to see his people grow in grace and truth.

As you work your way through this commentary and the letters of Paul to the Thessalonians, my prayer is that you will have a better grasp of how to study the Bible for yourself, as well as what questions to ask of the biblical text. Along with probing the Scriptures, I hope that you encounter the whole of Paul's argument as he wrote to a church that he loved deeply and didn't want to see them continue to be led astray by false teaching, which had stolen their assurance and joy. And as you grasp the big picture of each letter, I pray that the implications for your walk with Christ will become as clear as day.

Dr. Richard Bargas
Executive Director, IFCA International
Grand Rapids, MI

Introduction to
1 and 2 Thessalonians
on F.I.R.E.

Have you ever been misunderstood? Once I graduated from high school, I had no clue what to do vocationally. A friend guided me to apply for a job with a telephone company. This I did; two weeks later I found myself fully employed, making a weekly grand total of $153.50. The job consisted of typing documents for professional writers.

Although my typing skills would be enhanced—which helps greatly when you're a writer—my shyness hampered me. For instance, my boss gave me a nameplate. Instead of correctly spelling Ken Burge, it read "Ken Burg." Honestly, I'm not sure how this happened but the name appeared incorrect for more than one week. Eventually my boss caught the mistake and told me I should have revealed the right spelling of my name.

This embarrassed employee lived with his name being misunderstood for a brief period. Sadly, many well-meaning individuals don't grasp accurately the teachings in the Bible. My heart's desire consists of instructing truth-seekers to rightly divide the Word of truth.

This book, *1 and 2 Thessalonians on F.I.R.E.,* is an inductive commentary. This simply means that instead of telling you what the Bible teaches, it takes you on the journey to discover its life-changing communication. My goal is that you not only learn how to derive the meaning of the biblical text before you but also how to apply the message personally. My passion is to teach you how to develop the necessary skill set to become familiar with the Bible passage you are studying, interpret it accurately, relate it to its surrounding contexts, and employ it personally.

F.I.R.E. is the acronym used for our study. This mnemonic (memory) device stands for familiarity, interpretation, relationship, and employment. We will use all four of these steps each time we travel through a section of Scripture together.

F represents *familiarity*. Although I've been privileged to study the Bible at both the undergraduate and graduate levels, the emphasis was always upon observation as the first step of Bible study. My friend, doesn't that term seem cold and clinical versus the warmness expressed by familiarity? The Word of God shouldn't be placed under the microscope and scrutinized by those wearing white coats in a sterile environment.

The origin of the word "familiarity" derives from the Latin *familiaritas* and means "familiar" or "intimate." Bible study should originate from a deep-seated personal relationship with God. *Familiarity* roars out intimacy and relationship with the living God, while *observation* whimpers a frigid laboratory analysis of data.

Interpretation is the second stage of Bible study, represented here by the symbol **I**. Jesus has sent us a messenger to help us to understand the Scriptures—the eternal third member of the Godhead known as the Holy Spirit. Dependence upon Him is vital to enlighten our minds concerning God's truth. Jesus described the Holy Spirit as "the Spirit of truth" in John 16:13. He personally escorts us through the Bible, as the remainder of the verse says: "He will guide you into all truth."

Relationship is the third phase of our quest to understand the sacred text. The symbol **R** will stand for "relationship" throughout our travels. The Bible's value requires it to be treated with the utmost respect, "For the word of God is living and powerful, and sharper than any two-edged sword, piercing even to the division of soul and spirit, and of joints and marrow, and is a discerner of the thoughts and intents of the heart" (Heb. 4:12). We will see how the life-giving parts ally with the whole.

The fourth and final part of this most excellent adventure is *employment*, represented by the symbol **E**. Employment, or application, began when those who originally received the living Word were given their authoritative marching orders. We too will transition together, in order to determine not only how those to whom the Bible first came responded, but also how we are called to respond today. God designed His Word to transform us into the image of Christ, and that cannot occur without us first personally employing the Bible in our lives.

Now that you've been given an introduction to the tools we'll be using, let's embark together upon our study of *1 and 2 Thessalonians on F.I.R.E.*

BACKGROUND TO
1 AND 2 THESSALONIANS
ON F.I.R.E.

Paul and Silas established the church at Thessalonica, which today carries the name Thessaloniki or Salonika and is the second largest city in Greece, with a population around 400,000. In Paul's day Macedonia was the province in northern Greece that housed Thessalonica. Achaia existed in the southern region of Greece that contained the noteworthy cities of Athens and Corinth.

Luke documents Paul and Silas's ministry in Acts 17:1–10. Most likely Timothy was left at Philippi when Paul and Silas initially went to Thessalonica. Imagine the dedication to the ministry that Paul and Silas exhibit. They were beaten with rods in Philippi, put in the stocks (Acts 16:22–24), and then traveled one hundred miles to preach the gospel to those in Thessalonica.

The ministry commenced when "Paul, as his custom was, went in to them, and for three Sabbaths reasoned with them from the Scriptures" (Acts 17:2). Some believed (Acts 17:4), but Paul and Silas eventually were expelled from the city. How long did Paul and Silas remain in Thessalonica before being driven out?

One view states that Paul and Silas only spent three weeks total in Thessalonica (Acts 17:2). Yet Paul and Silas developed a significant Gentile ministry, which would have taken more time. Indeed, they had also fostered significant pastoral relationships (1 Thess. 2:1–8) and had received at least two separate financial gifts (Phil. 4:16), although Paul also supported himself through manual labor (1 Thess.

2:9). Most likely the committed tandem spent months in the city before being ousted.

Reading Luke's accounts in Acts 17–18 alongside of 1 Thessalonians points to Paul writing to the saints at Thessalonica from Corinth. An inscription found at Delphi (central Greece) calls Gallio proconsul of Achaia at the time Paul ministered at Corinth (Acts 18:12). Gallio is believed to have been the governor from July, AD 51–June, AD 52, and thus these details would place the time of writing around AD 51–52.

The apostle has at least three primary purposes in writing: first, to show his appreciation for the church's spiritual well-being (1 Thess. 1); next, to assure the church that he was fine after having to abruptly leave their city, and to clear up any misunderstanding about him and his associates (1 Thess. 2:1–3:10); and third, to encourage them to grow in holiness and their walk with the Lord (1 Thess. 3:11–5:28).

First Thessalonians can be divided in two parts. "Reflection from the Past" gives us the first major division of the letter (1 Thess. 1:1–3:13). "Requirements for the Future" then instructs the saints what to do based upon the apostle's reflection (1 Thess. 4:1–5:28).

Second Thessalonians has three divisions. "Continuing Despite Persecution" (2 Thess. 1:1–12) is the first. Next, "Clarifying the Day of Christ" covers chapter two (2 Thess. 2:1–17). Finally, "Closing Exhortation to the Saints" is the third division (2 Thess. 3:1–18).

Prayerfully let's depend upon the Spirit of God to guide us through 1 and 2 Thessalonians.

PART ONE

REFLECTION FROM THE PAST

1 Thessalonians 1:1–3:13

CHAPTER ONE

WHAT SHOULD CHRISTIAN MODELS DISPLAY?

1 Thessalonians 1:1–4

A police officer pulls over a driver and asks for his license and registration. "What's wrong officer?" the driver asks. "I didn't go through any red lights, and I wasn't speeding."

"No, you weren't," said the officer, "but I saw you waving your fist at another driver and then shouting at the motorist who cut you off."

"Is that a crime, officer?"

"No, but when I saw the 'Jesus loves you and so do I' bumper sticker on the car, I figured this car had to be stolen."

Sadly, the message on the bumper sticker did not match the character of the driver. Thankfully, the lives of the believers we are about to study align with the bumper sticker's motto.

Each passage we study will be introduced with two Bible translations. First, I use the New King James Version (NKJV), with each text followed by one of three different translations. Please read both translations carefully and prayerfully to prepare for the study.

Paul, Silvanus, and Timothy,

To the church of the Thessalonians in God the Father and the Lord Jesus Christ:

Grace to you and peace from God our Father and the Lord Jesus Christ.

We give thanks to God always for you all, making mention of you in our prayers, remembering without ceasing your work of faith, labor of love, and patience of hope in our Lord Jesus Christ in the sight of our God and Father, knowing, beloved brethren, your election by God. (1 Thess. 1–4)

From Paul, Silas, and Timothy,

To the church in Thessalonica, the people of God the Father and of the Lord Jesus Christ.

I pray that God will be kind to you and will bless you with peace!

We thank God for you and always mention you in our prayers. Each time we pray, we tell God our Father about your faith and loving work and about your firm hope in our Lord Jesus Christ.

My dear friends, God loves you, and we know he has chosen you to be his people. (1 Thess. 1–4, CEV)

MODELING FAITH, HOPE, AND LOVE – F

- Who are Paul, Silvanus, and Timothy (v. 1)?
- What do the terms "grace" and "peace" mean (v. 1)?
- How important are faith, hope, and love to a church (v. 3)?
- Why does Paul write about "your election by God" (v. 4)?

MODELING FAITH, HOPE, AND LOVE – I

The author of the epistle self-identifies as Paul; although he becomes a giant in the faith, his Greek name means "little." Formerly as a Pharisee he persecuted the church of Jesus Christ (Acts 9:1–2; 1 Tim. 1:12–13). Dramatically he was saved through a post-resurrection appearance of Jesus (Acts 9:3–6), which qualified him to be an apostle—and the last person to see the Lord (1 Cor. 15:8).

Paul does not call himself an apostle or a bondservant of Christ in 1 and 2 Thessalonians. Most likely he leaves off these descriptive terms because the saints warmly embrace him and submit to his leadership. The apostle follows the model set by Jesus to minister with others (see Luke 10 and the sending of the seventy). "Two are better than one," writes Solomon, "Because they have a good reward for their labor. For if they fall, one will lift up his companion. But woe to him who is alone when he falls, for he has no one to help him up" (Eccl. 4:9–10). Paul ministers alongside of Silvanus and Timothy; therefore, he simultaneously trains them and enjoys their fellowship.

Luke regularly chooses the name "Silas" to describe Paul's companion, which seems to be used in Jewish circles (Acts 15:22–40; 16:19–20); while Paul and Peter prefer "Silvanus," which appears to be used in Hellenistic settings (2 Cor. 1:19; 2 Thess. 1:1). Peter labels him a "faithful brother" (1 Pet. 5:12) and his stellar reputation enables him to be dispatched to the Jerusalem council (Acts 15:22–33). Moreover he is cited as a preacher to the trustworthy Word of God (2 Cor. 1:19) and a prophet (Acts 15:32). He becomes Paul's traveling companion after Mark's departure (Acts 16:11–40).

The name "Timothy" means *one who honors or values God* and emerges twenty-four times from the Greek New Testament. His name first appears in Acts 16. "Then he [Paul] came to Derbe and Lystra. And behold, a certain disciple was there, named Timothy, the son of a certain Jewish woman who believed, but his father was Greek. He was well spoken of by the brethren who were at Lystra and Iconium" (Acts 16:1–2). Paul warmly identifies him as "my fellow worker" (Rom. 16:21), "our brother" (2 Cor. 1:1), a fellow bondservant (Phil. 1:1), and "a true son in the faith" (1 Tim. 1:2). Affectionately he also describes him as "a beloved son" (2 Tim. 1:2). Both Silas and Timothy are quality disciples!

Location is often cited as the most important feature of real estate. Church planters also value a well-placed church to reach the masses. As Paul addresses "the church of the Thessalonians," we should note that during the apostle's day this was the largest and most important city in Macedonia, where also the capital of the province resided. Situated between the Adriatic and the Hellespont at the head of the Thermaic Gulf along with a notable harbor with renown trade routes made for a strategically placed church.

The church at Thessalonica is "in God the Father and the Lord Jesus Christ." Father and Son are closely associated in 1 and 2 Thessalonians (1 Thess. 3:11–13; 5:18; 2 Thess. 1:1, 2, 8, 12; 2:16; 3:5). Clearly Paul's positioning of Father and Son recognizes the equality of their deity.

Paul bestows his customary greeting: "Grace to you and peace from God our Father and the Lord Jesus Christ." The term "grace," which occurs 156 times in the Greek New Testament, means *favor*. Observe that God's "grace" or "favor" appears before "peace." God's grace must first be experienced before knowing His peace. The former Hebrew term *Shalom* gives us the background to the Greek word "peace." It refers to a fullness of physical and spiritual prosperity whereas the Greek word goes beyond and grants us a superior peace that "surpasses all understanding" (Phil. 4:7).

Next, Paul writes, "we give thanks to God always for you all" (v. 2). The compound verb translated "we give thanks" appears thirty-nine times. Literally it consists of *well* or *good* and *to grant*, so combined it communicates *to grant what is good*. Paul uses it far more often than any other New Testament writer. (Here is a partial listing: Romans 1:8, 21; 1 Corinthians 1:4; 2 Corinthians 1:11; Ephesians 1:16; 5:20; Philippians 1:3; Colossians 1:3, 12; 2 Thessalonians 1:3; 2:13; Philemon 4.) Paul personally practices what he exhorts others to do. Later in this letter he commands, "in everything give thanks; for this is the will of God in Christ Jesus for you" (1 Thess. 5:18).

Not only does Paul consistently give thanks, but he lifts up these saints in prayer to the throne of grace. He shares that he is "making mention of you in our prayers." The noun "mention" imparts *to recollect* and *to remember*. He uses one of the seven occurrences of this term in Philippians 1:3–4, stating, "I thank my God upon every remembrance of you, always in every prayer of mine making request for you all with joy."

Again, the man of God practices what he prescribes. Toward the end of this epistle Paul commands the saints to "pray without ceasing" (1 Thess. 5:17). Yet we shouldn't be surprised to know that he regularly bends his knees in their behalf. We should be encouraged that the Lord honors prayers of people like us! James writes, "Elijah was a man with a nature like ours, and he prayed earnestly that it would not rain; and it did not rain on the land for three years and six months" (James 5:17).

There are three things in particular that Paul recalls (the participle "remembering" being in the present tense shows a continual *bearing in mind* and the adverb "without ceasing" intensifies the recalling) about these believers (1 Thess. 1:3). He shares that he is "remembering without ceasing your work of faith, labor of love, and patience of hope." (The importance for the church having faith, hope, and love will be probed in the "relationship" section.)

A "work of faith" isn't a conflict of terms, but rather the descriptive genitive ("of faith") characterizes the kind of work. First, it is impossible to please the Lord without faith (Heb. 11:6). Indeed, faith becomes a must for the individual to apply concerning salvation (Eph. 2:8–9). Abraham's (James 2:22–23) and Rahab's (James 2:24-26) works displayed their genuine salvation.

Besides having a "work of faith," secondly the saints displayed a "labor of love." Once again a descriptive genitive ("of love") depicts the kind of "labor." Paul's term "labor" refers *to working to the point of fatigue*; the noun emerges nineteen times from the Greek New Testament. The sacrificial apostle declares his love for these saints when he uses the same term, writing, "For you remember, brethren, our labor and toil; for laboring night and day, that we might not be a burden to any of you" (1 Thess. 2:9).

Also, every Christian will be judged based upon his or her own labor in ministry. "Now he who plants and he who waters are one," writes Paul to the Corinthians, "and each one will receive his own reward according to his own labor" (1 Cor. 3:8). Brothers and sisters, don't forget "that your labor is not in vain in the Lord" (1 Cor. 15:58), and "God is not unjust to forget your work and labor of love which you have shown toward His name, in that you have ministered to the saints, and do minister" (Heb. 6:10).

The third in a series of descriptive genitives is "of hope," found in the expression "patience of hope." Children of God have a *steadfast endurance*, which is the meaning of "patience," portrayed as hopeful. "Patience" derives from the preposition *under* and *to remain*. Saints are *to remain under* their trials because of the hope of Jesus' imminent return. Paul characterizes the Rapture as "one hope of your calling" (Eph. 4:4). He extends that comforting hope to the persecuted Thessalonian saints (1 Thess. 1:6, 10).

Both Father and Son have observed the service of the saints for Paul writes that these things are "in our Lord Jesus Christ in the sight of our God and Father." To be in the "sight of" implies the knowledge of God over the work of ministry. To each of the seven churches in Asia Minor Jesus says, "I know your works" (Rev. 2:2, 9, 13, 19; 3:1, 8, 15). When the Lord Jesus returns for His church the saints will be rewarded for their faithful service; God never forgets (Heb. 6:10).

Only the Lord possesses a full knowledge of everything, but Paul also understands something very important about these saints. He offers, "knowing, beloved brethren, your election by God" (1 Thess. 1:4). He desires the Thessalonians to fully perceive that they are true believers. After all, God chose them before Adam and Eve walked on planet earth. "Just as He [God] chose us in Him [Jesus] before the foundation of the world, that we should be holy and without blame before Him in love" (Eph. 1:4), pens the grateful apostle!

MODELING FAITH, HOPE, AND LOVE – R

Faith, hope, and love when applied in the saint's life or employed by any church showcases Christian maturity. These three character qualities surface from the lives of the Thessalonian believers. Observe the triad: "remembering without ceasing your work of faith, labor of love, and patience of hope in our Lord Jesus Christ in the sight of our God and Father" (1 Thess. 1:3). Interestingly, the apostle declares that the church of Thessalonica is a model congregation: "And you became followers of us and of the Lord, having received the word in much

26

affliction, with joy of the Holy Spirit, so that you became examples to all in Macedonia and Achaia who believe" (1 Thess. 1:6–7).

Even mature individuals or churches need to continue developing in these three areas. "But let us who are of the day be sober," pens the spiritual father of these saints, "putting on the breastplate of faith and love, and as a helmet the hope of salvation" (1 Thess. 5:8). Yet misinformation (see 2 Thess. 2:1–2) caused these quality saints to lose one facet of the essential triad: hope. They fall victim to erroneous information and for this reason believe they missed the Rapture, which is their blessed hope. As a result Paul leaves out "hope" in the greeting with his second epistle to them. "We are bound to thank God always for you, brethren, as it is fitting, because your faith grows exceedingly, and the love of every one of you all abounds toward each other" (2 Thess. 1:3). Paul labors to restore their hope by correcting the fallacy imparted to them!

Paul writes the letters to the Thessalonians from Corinth. God had gifted these saints with all the spiritual gifts (1 Cor. 1:7); however, they abuse the priorities of their giftedness and the apostle corrects them (1 Cor. 12:1–14:40). The apostle to the Gentiles makes the argument that spiritual gifts are temporal, whereas love is eternal. That is why he makes a series of overstatements (hyperbole) in 1 Corinthians 13:1–3. In essence, he says, you can have extraordinary gifts, but if you lack love you have nothing. Continuing his correction of the saints Paul articulates, "And now abide faith, hope, love, these three, but the greatest of these is love" (1 Cor. 13:13). Note the singular verb "abide" that shows the unity of faith, hope, and love. Wisely, and by inspiration of the Holy Spirit, the apostle shows the importance of having faith, hope, and love.

Maturing saints have a close relationship with the church of Jesus Christ. The Lord gave gifted men to the church to equip believers (Eph. 4:11–16). Moreover, the writer of Hebrews refers to faith, hope, and love in connection with attending church (Heb. 10:22–25). He writes, "let us draw near [to God] with a true heart in full assurance of faith" (v. 22). Next, "let us hold fast the confession of our hope without wavering" (v. 23). "And let us consider one another in order to stir up love and good works" (v. 24). He culminates with "not forsaking the assembling of ourselves together, as is the manner of some, but exhorting one another, and so much the more as you see the Day approaching" (v. 25). Christians are not called to be lone rangers, but to grow together in faith, hope, and love.

MODELING FAITH, HOPE, AND LOVE – E

Model Christian maturity by exhibiting faith, hope, and love is our employment point. Faith can be defined as taking God at His Word and acting upon it. You are to memorize, meditate, and seek to act upon Hebrews 11:6, which says, "But without faith it is impossible to please Him, for he who comes to God must believe that He is, and that He is a rewarder of those who diligently seek Him." Like the heroes of faith, believe the promises in the Bible and employ them to your life.

Next, reflect upon Titus 2:13, which reveals that we are to be "looking for the blessed hope and glorious appearing of our great God and Savior Jesus Christ." Contrary to the exhortations of many, we are not to be looking for signs concerning the Rapture. Rather, we are to be anticipating the imminent return of Jesus Christ and actively serving Him while we wait.

Finally, read 1 Corinthians 13:4–8a each day. Paul describes love as follows: "Love suffers long and is kind; love does not envy; love does not parade itself, is not puffed up; does not behave rudely, does not seek its own, is not provoked, thinks no evil; does not rejoice in iniquity, but rejoices in the truth; bears all things, believes all things, hopes all things, endures all things. Love never fails." Seven days of reading this passage should give it plenty of time to settle into your soul.

Remember, *model Christian maturity by exhibiting faith, hope, and love*. Let us become like the saints at Thessalonica, who became an example to the world in which they lived!

CHAPTER TWO

DO YOU HAVE CREDIBLE WITNESS TO YOUR ELECTION?

1 Thessalonians 1:5–10

Tom was in the hospital, near death. The family called their pastor to be with him. As the pastor stood next to the bed, Tom's condition appeared to deteriorate and he motioned frantically for something to write on. The pastor lovingly handed him a pen and a piece of paper, and Tom used his last bit of energy to scribble a note, then died.

The pastor thought it best not to look at the note at that time, so he placed it in his jacket pocket. At the funeral, as he was finishing the message, he realized that he was wearing the same jacket he was wearing when Tom died. He said, "You know, Tom handed me a note just before he died. I haven't looked at it, but knowing Tom, I'm sure it's a wonderful message." He opened the note, and read, "Get off my oxygen tube!"

Tom's pastor desired to testify of his parishioner's Christian life that he was truly one of God's elect; however, that witness was cut off. How many credible witnesses do you have concerning your election?

Let's slow down to thoughtfully read our passage with two different Bible translations.

For our gospel did not come to you in word only, but also in power, and in the Holy Spirit and in much assurance, as you know what kind of men we were among you for your sake.

And you became followers of us and of the Lord, having received the word in much affliction, with joy of the Holy Spirit, so that you became examples to all in Macedonia and Achaia who believe. For from you the word of the Lord has sounded forth, not only in Macedonia and Achaia, but also in every place. Your faith toward God has gone out, so that we do not need to say anything. For they themselves declare concerning us what manner of entry we had to you, and how you turned to God from idols to serve the living and true God, and to wait for His Son from heaven, whom He raised from the dead, even Jesus who delivers us from the wrath to come. (1 Thess. 1:5–10)

For our gospel did not come to you in word only, but also in power and in the Holy Spirit and with full conviction; just as you know what kind of men we proved to be among you for your sake. You also became imitators of us and of the Lord, having received the word in much tribulation with the joy of the Holy Spirit, so that you became an example to all the believers in Macedonia and in Achaia. For the word of the Lord has sounded forth from you, not only in Macedonia and Achaia, but also in every place your faith toward God has gone forth, so that we have no need to say anything. For they themselves report about us what kind of reception we had with you, and how you turned to God from idols to serve a living and true God, and to wait for His Son from heaven, whom He raised from the dead, that is Jesus, who rescues us from the wrath to come. (1 Thess. 1:5–10, NASB)

Can I Get a Witness? – F

- What relationship does "for" (v. 5) have with "your election by God" (v. 4)?

- What three evidences does Paul cite about proclaiming the gospel (v. 5)?

- Why does Paul place "followers of us" before "and of the Lord" (v. 6)?

- How can the believer have "much affliction, with joy of the Holy Spirit" (v. 6)?
- What key theological term describes the second half of verse 9?
- How does 1 Thessalonians 1:10 demonstrate the Rapture before the Tribulation?

CAN I GET A WITNESS? – I

The conjunction "for" has been understood variously. Some believe that it is epexegetical, which means that Paul is giving additional information (vv. 5–10) on election (v. 4). This view interprets the remaining chapter (vv. 5–10) as giving further clarification as to the nature of the saints' election. It is better to understand the conjunction "for" as causal. In other words, Paul is articulating his rationale for comprehending that the Thessalonians are elect; he is not portraying wherein their election consisted.

The apostle presents two arguments testifying to the election of the Thessalonians. Paul's first reason confirming the Thessalonians' election is his, Timothy, and Silas's testimony (v. 5). His second explanation confirming the Thessalonians' election is their testimony and expansive witness (vv. 6–10).

"For our gospel did not come to you in word only," writes Paul (v. 5). The gospel was presented with words, yes, but more than mere words. Paul, Silas, and Timothy personalized Jesus' death, burial, and resurrection. After being beaten with rods and put in the stocks at Philippi (Acts 16:22–24; 1 Thess. 2:2), Paul and Silas traveled approximately one hundred miles to preach the gospel in Thessalonica. The compound term "gospel" surfaces seventy-seven times from the Greek New Testament and conveys *to proclaim good news*.

The following three aspects of the gospel are shared: "in power and in the Holy Spirit and in much assurance." Paul uses the singular noun "power" that means *ability, achieving power*, which term he applies in Romans 1:16, "For I am not ashamed of the gospel of Christ, for it is the power of God to salvation for everyone who believes."

"In the Holy Spirit" refers to the convicting ministry of the third person of the Trinity. Jesus says about the Helper, "And when He has come, He will convict the world of sin, and of righteousness, and of judgment" (John 16:8). Thirdly, the gospel arrived "in much assurance." The feminine noun "assurance" refers to a *perfect certitude, full assurance,* or *complete understanding.* These saints grasped their need to believe in the finished work of Christ. Clearly Paul and his associates sensed God moving in the hearts of these saints for salvation.

The apostle then appeals to the recollection of the Thessalonian believers, "as you know what kind of men we were among you for your sake." These recent converts not only are recipients of a powerful message, but also witnessed well-lived servants of Jesus whose talk is confirmed by their walk. (More details on this subject will be forthcoming in 1 Thessalonians 2.)

"And you became followers of us and of the Lord," writes Paul (1 Thess. 1:6). Fascinatingly Paul places "followers of us" prior to "the Lord." What a great reminder that the unsaved first see us! We are to be the ushers to bring the lost to Jesus. "Followers" occurs seven times from the Greek New Testament and speaks of being *an imitator* or *mimicker.* First Corinthians 4:16 shares the apostle's words, "Therefore I urge you, imitate me." Then later in the same epistle he offers, "Imitate me, just as I also imitate Christ" (1 Cor. 11:1). Firsthand the Thessalonian saints observe the life of Paul and Silas, and eventually Timothy, and are drawn to Jesus.

Paradox describes the lives of the Thessalonian saints, "having received the word in much affliction, with joy of the Holy Spirit." Thankfully these lost souls received with open arms that which Paul and Silas offered them. The participle "having received" reveals that a welcome mat is placed in front of the homes of those who believed the powerful gospel message. Luke uses the same term of Jesus describing the mission of the seventy, "whatever city you enter, and they receive you, eat such things as are set before you" (Luke 10:8). Again

32

he chooses the same term in Acts 17:11 of the Bereans: "in that they received the word with all readiness."

However, the Thessalonians paid a price, as those welcoming the Word "in much affliction." *To crush, press, compress, squeeze* imparts the literal meaning of the term "affliction." Figuratively the word conveys *pressure from wickedness, affliction, and distress.* Paul presents a similar paradox about joy while under pressure in Romans 12:12: "rejoicing in hope, patient in tribulation." Jesus previously warned His followers to expect this world's system to distress them: "These things I have spoken to you, that in Me you may have peace. In the world you will have tribulation; but be of good cheer, I have overcome the world" (John 16:33). Thankfully the Thessalonians imitate Paul, Silas, and Timothy in enduring these pressures (1 Thess. 3:3, 7).

The second fruit of the Holy Spirit (joy), as mentioned in Galatians 5:22, describes the saints at Thessalonica. Although they experience "much affliction," they also are "with joy of the Holy Spirit." Their hope in the Lord while anticipating His imminent return helps enable them to endure severe trials. Paul's wish for the Roman believers (and all the saints) comes true for these children of God. "Now may the God of hope fill you with all joy and peace in believing, that you may abound in hope by the power of the Holy Spirit" (Rom. 15:13).

Paul chronicles the result of the saints embracing the gospel even though they are persecuted. He writes, "so that you became examples to all in Macedonia and Achaia who believe" (1 Thess. 1:7). "So that" derives from a Greek structure referring to result; their powerful testimony results in being "examples" to all of Greece (Macedonia and Achaia) who have placed their faith in Jesus Christ. The Greek term "examples" means *to strike repeatedly* and the figurative use in our passage directs us *to a pattern or example to be imitated.*

"For from you the word of the Lord has sounded forth," notes Paul, "not only in Macedonia and Achaia, but also in every place" (v. 8). The perfect tense verb "has sounded forth" shows a *sounding abroad* in the past with the results continuing. A clap of thunder, or a radio signal that keeps advancing, gives the idea of the term. Reverberations of the saints' lives transcend ancient Macedonia and Achaia, having a broader impact. Paul uses a hyperbole (overstatement), "in every place," to communicate the far-reaching testimony of these committed Christians.

Paul continues his hyperbole with the following: "Your faith toward God has gone out, so that we do not need to say anything." Not only did these saints readily receive the message of the gospel but they also dispatched it globally. Paul, Silas, and Timothy had to be monumentally pleased with the receptivity and sharing of the death, burial, and resurrection of Jesus!

It isn't Paul and his companions of ministry who are giving these reports but travelers who visit Corinth, testifying about the Thessalonians. Gladly Paul proclaims, "For they themselves declare concerning us what manner of entry we had to you, and how you turned to God from idols to serve the living and true God" (v. 9). "Declaring" is composed of the preposition meaning *from* and the verb meaning *to tell or declare*. The present tense depicts the continual telling of the missionaries' service to the Thessalonians.

Repentance best describes the theology behind Paul's words. He marvels, "and how you turned to God from idols to serve the living and true God." Paul uses the aorist (past) tense "you turned" to paint a picture of people held captive by dead idols now moving in the totally opposite direction. He transitions from the past tense verb "you turned" to the present infinitive (verbal noun) "to serve" touting the movement from one master in the past to presently serving another. Jesus declared the impossibility of equally being in bondage to two owners. He said, "No one can serve two masters" (Matt. 6:24). These former captives of Satan through the mechanism of idolatry now are joyously serving "the living and true God." Both Father (John 17:3) and Jesus (1 John 5:20) are declared to be the true God!

Paul concludes the first chapter with, "and to wait for His Son from heaven, whom He raised from the dead, even Jesus who delivers us from the wrath to come" (v. 10). "To wait" consists of a preposition used as an intensifier and the verb *to remain*. The present tense infinitive shows a continuous and strong anticipation. Jesus is "the Son of Him," which is the literal translation of "His Son." Their focus remains upward, since the Lord will return "from heaven." Biblically the term "heaven" or "heavens" has a range of meaning. For example, it can refer to the sky. Jesus says in Matthew 6:26, "look at the birds of the air" (literally "of the heaven"). Paul, most likely referring to himself, pens, "such a one was caught up to the third heaven" (2 Cor. 12:2), which is heaven proper. Then the term occurs four times in Acts 1:9–11 of Jesus ascending to heaven. As Jesus went to heaven, He will return from the same location!

Our author next gives strong emphasis to who conquered death, when he writes, "whom He raised from the dead," and then identifies the risen Lord as "even Jesus who delivers us from the wrath to come." *To draw* or *drag along the ground* gives us the meaning of "delivers." It is used of someone being drawn or snatched from danger. The middle voice verb shows that God rescues us for His own purposes.

Jesus delivers the saints for His own designs "from the wrath to come." The word "wrath" points *to anger as a state of mind*. As we will see under relationship, the wrath consists of both the wrath of the Tribulation and eternal damnation.

CAN I GET A WITNESS? – R

Will the church-age saint enter the Tribulation as described in Revelation 6–19? If you believe that Jesus returns for the church prior to the Tribulation, then you hold to a pretribulation Rapture; however, if you maintain the view that the Rapture occurs after the Tribulation, then you belong to the camp of a posttribulation Rapture. I will first show from our current passage why I believe the Rapture happens before the Tribulation, and that Jesus' Second Coming to the earth after the Tribulation is separate, as revealed in Revelation 19:11–21.

I believe Paul affirms a pretribulational Rapture in 1 Thessalonians 1:10. Taking Paul's words at face value about "Jesus who delivers us from the wrath to come" argues strongly for the Rapture prior to the Tribulation! Paul's term "delivers" can refer to a spiritual (Col. 1:13; 2 Pet. 2:9) or physical (Matt. 27:43; 2 Cor. 1:10) deliverance. Peter describes the extrication of Lot from Sodom with this term (2 Pet. 2:7). Clearly the concept is that of a physical and bodily deliverance before the destruction of Sodom. The apostle's choice of "delivers" in conjunction "from the wrath to come" has a similar application to that of Lot from the wicked Sodom.

We will probe two aspects of "wrath." The first consists of the wrath of the Tribulation. John characterizes the commencement of the Tribulation as follows: "For the great day of His wrath has come, and who is able to stand?" (Revelation 6:17). God's apostle on the isle of Patmos states unequivocally that the period of the Tribulation is a time of wrath. First Thessalonians makes the case that the saints do not enter this period of wrath (1 Thess. 1:10; 5:9). Later in 1 Thessalonians Paul declares, "for God did not appoint us to wrath, but to obtain salvation through our Lord Jesus Christ" (1 Thess. 5:9). Again, the deliverance occurs before the Tribulation.

To the church of Philadelphia Jesus teaches, "Because you have kept My command to persevere, I also will keep you from the hour of trial which shall come upon the whole world" (Rev. 3:10). What Jesus teaches one church applies to all churches, because He says, "He who has an ear, let him hear what the Spirit says to the churches" (Rev. 3:13; 2:7, 11, 17; 29; 3:6, 3:22). We are promised that we won't enter "the hour of trial which will come upon the whole world," which refers to the Tribulation.

Finally, seven times Jesus says, "He who has an ear, let him hear what the Spirit says to the churches" (see above references). Yet after the Tribulation begins (Rev. 6), John records, "If anyone has an ear, let him hear" (Rev. 13:9). He deliberately leaves off the words, "what the Spirit says to the churches"—because the church has been removed before the Tribulation.

Paul and John are equally on the same theological page and teach that the Rapture happens prior to the Tribulation. Now let's transition to putting into practice what we've learned from 1 Thessalonians 1:5–10.

CAN I GET A WITNESS? – E

Would your spiritual leaders testify to your election based upon your life? Moreover, if you are put on trial as a Christian, would your testimony hold true in a court of law? *Confirm your election through your leaders' testimony* is our first employment point. Paul, Silas, and Timothy could all give testimony under oath about the positive spiritual lives of the saints at Thessalonica. I want you to set up an appointment to speak with one if not two of your spiritual leaders. Then, with boldness and humility, ask them to assess your life spiritually.

Remember, "obey those who rule over you, and be submissive, for they watch out for your souls, as those who must give account. Let them do so with joy and not with grief, for that would be unprofitable for you" (Heb. 13:17). God has placed you under spiritual heads, so take the time and let them either affirm or disaffirm your Christian walk.

The saints at Thessalonica have a strong testimony not only among their leaders, but all those who knew them. *Confirm your election through your testimony* is our second employment point. Determine with God's help and by His grace to lead a life worthy of imitation. Prayerfully read the following verses and dedicate yourself to becoming like the believers at Thessalonica who had a local and global reach:

And you became followers of us and of the Lord, having received the word in much affliction, with joy of the Holy Spirit, so that you became examples to all in Macedonia and Achaia who believe. For from you the world of the Lord has sounded forth, not only in Macedonia and Achaia, but also in every place. Your faith toward God has gone out, so that we do not need to say anything. (vv. 6–8)

CHAPTER THREE

BE A SELF-SACRIFICING, HAPPY HERALD

1 Thessalonians 2:1–12

Some members of a congregation approach their pastor about trouble in the church. Airing their grievances, they make multiple charges against those with whom they are at odds. Responding to the complaints the minister says, "You're right. You are absolutely right."

The next night, however, another group comes to his home and tell their side of the story. He listens very quietly, and when they had finished, said, "You're right. You are absolutely right."

His wife, working in the kitchen, overhears everything. As soon as the members leave, she rushes into the living room and exclaims, "You are just about the most wishy-washy individual I've ever seen!"

To which he responds, "You're right. You are absolutely right!"

Paul, unlike this wishy-washy pastor, modeled a life of integrity to the Thessalonians. He and his like-minded associates could appeal to the saints at Thessalonica to imitate them and live for Jesus. Here are a couple of questions for you to ponder before reading the passage: What does the Lord expect from those who share the gospel? Also, how should you act when sharing the gospel?

For you yourselves know, brethren, that our coming to you was not in vain. But even after we had suffered before and were spitefully treated at Philippi, as you know, we were bold in our God to speak to you the gospel of God in much conflict. For our exhortation did not come from error or uncleanness, nor was it in deceit.

But as we have been approved by God to be entrusted with the gospel, even so we speak, not as pleasing men, but God who tests our hearts. For neither at any time did we use flattering words, as you know, nor a cloak for covetousness—God is witness. Nor did we seek glory from men, either from you or from others, when we might have made demands as apostles of Christ. But we were gentle among you, just as a nursing mother cherishes her own children. So, affectionately longing for you, we were well pleased to impart to you not only the gospel of God, but also our own lives, because you had become dear to us. For you remember, brethren, our labor and toil; for laboring night and day, that we might not be a burden to any of you, we preached to you the gospel of God.

You are witnesses, and God also, how devoutly and justly and blamelessly we behaved ourselves among you who believe; as you know how we exhorted, and comforted, and charged every one of you, as a father does his own children, that you would walk worthy of God who calls you into His own kingdom and glory. (1 Thess. 2:1–12)

You know, brothers and sisters, that our visit to you was not without results. We had previously suffered and been treated outrageously in Philippi, as you know, but with the help of our God we dared to tell you his gospel in the face of strong opposition. For the appeal we make does not spring from error or impure motives, nor are we trying to trick you. On the contrary, we speak as those approved by God to be entrusted with the gospel. We are not trying to please people but God, who tests our hearts. You know we never used flattery, nor did we put on a mask to cover up greed—God is our witness. We were not looking for praise from people, not from you or anyone else, even though as apostles of Christ we could have asserted our authority. Instead, we were like young children among you.

Just as a nursing mother cares for her children, so we cared for you. Because we loved you so much, we were delighted to share with you not only the gospel of God but our lives as well. Surely you remember, brothers and sisters, our toil and hardship; we worked night and day in order not to be a burden to anyone while we preached the gospel of God to you. You are witnesses, and so is God, of how holy, righteous and blameless we were among you who believed. For you know that we dealt with each of you as a father deals with his own children, encouraging, comforting and urging you to live lives worthy of God, who calls you into his kingdom and glory. (1 Thess. 2:1–12. NIV)

HEAR YE, HEAR YE, GOSPEL HERALDS – F

- How are Paul and Silas "spitefully treated at Philippi" (v. 2)?
- What three things didn't Paul and Silas practice (v. 3)?
- What is the result of being pleasers of men (v. 4)?
- What "demands as apostles of Christ" could Paul have made (v. 6)?
- Why does Paul describe the missionary team "as a nursing mother" (v. 7)?
- How do Paul, Silas, and Timothy imitate Jesus (v. 8)?
- What three adverbs does Paul use to describe integrity (v. 10)?
- Why does Paul describe the missionary team "as a father" (v. 11)?

HEAR YE, HEAR YE, GOSPEL HERALDS – I

"For you yourselves know, brethren, that our coming to you was not in vain" (v. 1). The "for" connects chapters two and three as an expansion of Paul's and Silas's "coming" with 1 Thessalonians 1:9. (The same verb "coming" from 2:1 is translated "entry" in 1:9.) Emphatically the apostle employs "you yourselves" and then adds the word "know." He uses "you know" regularly in the current chapter (2:1, 2, 5, 11). On four occasions Paul appeals to the knowledge of the Thessalonians as to Silas, Timothy, and his own integrity.

"Know" doesn't give us the term that refers to *experiential knowledge* (*ginosko*), but *fullness of knowledge* (*oida*). To unbelievers, Jesus says concerning the Father, "Yet you have not known [the Greek term that is *not* used in our passage for experiential knowledge] Him, but I know [the same word used in verse 1 pointing to a fullness of knowledge] Him" (John 8:55).

"Brethren," which denotes *from the same womb,* appears nineteen times in 1 Thessalonians, reminding us frequently that believers are eternally linked as blood-bought brothers and sisters in Christ. Paul and Silas made quite an "entry." The word "entry" (1:9), translated "coming" in 1 Thessalonians 2:1, communicates *unto a road or way* (occurring five times from the Greek New Testament). Indeed, the visit "was not in vain." Eighteen times the adjective "vain" emerges, meaning *empty* or *hollow;* biblically speaking, it reflects the idea of *fruitless.* Certainly Paul and Silas bore eternal fruit with their bold entrance to Thessalonica.

"But even after we had suffered before and were spitefully treated at Philippi," continues the apostle (v. 2). Paul's and Silas's wounds are still fresh as they fiercely proclaimed the gospel in Thessalonica. "We had suffered before" derives from a compound term found only here from the Greek. The dynamic tandem had not only previously suffered but "were spitefully treated at Philippi." Five times "spitefully treated" appears in the Greek New Testament. The first use comes from Matthew 22:6 from Jesus' parable of the wedding banquet: "And the rest seized his servants, treated them spitefully, and killed them." Sadly, Paul and Silas are similarly abused (although not killed) in Philippi (see Acts 16:16–26). Paul appeals to the knowledge ("as you know") of the Thessalonians for a second time.

Nevertheless, the apostle stresses, "we were bold in our God to speak to you the gospel of God in much conflict." The expression "we were bold" comes from a compound verb literally meaning *all speech,* which conveys *a freedom or boldness of speech.* The first two times the verb surfaces is recorded by Luke, when Barnabas tells the Christians who doubted Paul's conversion about his bold preaching (Acts 9:27,

29). Years later, the apostle tenaciously and courageously heralds the gospel after many afflictions.

Although the apostle traveled extensively his message remains the same. God gave him the courage "to speak to you the gospel of God in much conflict." Out of the seventy–seven uses in the New Testament of "gospel," six of those emerge in 1 Thessalonians (1:5; 2:2, 4, 8, 9; 3:2). The proclamation came "in much conflict." Paul's analogy comes from the Greek games where the term refers to running, boxing, and wrestling. Appropriately, the apostle uses the picturesque term in Philippians 1:30 referring to an outer conflict: "having the same conflict which you saw in me and now hear in me." Paul chooses the same word to refer to an inner conflict he had for the never-seen Colossian saints (Col. 2:1). Toward the end of his ministry he exhorts the saints, "Fight the good fight ("conflict") of faith" (1 Tim. 6:12), and culminates with "I have fought the good fight" ("conflict") in 2 Timothy 4:7.

A defense of the ministry continues concerning the integrity of Paul, Silas, and Timothy. First, Paul uses three negatives to argue his case (v. 3), followed by the positive (v. 4). "For our exhortation did not come from error or uncleanness, nor was it in deceit," writes Paul. All three missionaries *come alongside of*—the literal meaning of "exhortation"—the Thessalonian saints. First, their exhortation, as negatively stated, "did not come from error." *Wandering from the right path* conveys the meaning of the figurative use of "error" given here.

Next, the disciples didn't display "uncleanness" to the saints. Jesus is the first to use the term as recorded in Matthew 23:27, when He says to the scribes and Pharisees, "For you are like whitewashed tombs which indeed appear beautiful outwardly, but inwardly are full of dead men's bones and all uncleanness." Also, "uncleanness" appears among the works of the flesh in Galatians 5:19. Perhaps Paul hints at the sexual immorality traveling peddlers of religion practiced (1 Thess. 2:3).

Third, "nor was it in deceit," declares Paul. "Deceit" used literally means *to bait,* and its metaphorical meaning here indicates *deceit, fraud*, and *guile*. Matthew gives us the first use of the word about the chief priests, scribes, and elders who "plotted to take Jesus by trickery [deceit] and kill Him" (Matt. 26:4). Peter, an experienced fisherman, applies the term: "Therefore, laying aside all malice, all deceit, hypocrisy, envy, and all evil speaking" (1 Pet. 2:1).

Positively, then, the apostle states the following: "But as we have been approved by God to be entrusted with the gospel, even so we speak, not as pleasing men, but God who tests our hearts" (v. 4). The adversative "but" gives the contrast from the prior verse (v. 3) with its three negatives. Paul's use of the perfect tense verb "have been approved" passes on the concept that they "have been approved by God to be entrusted with the gospel" in the past and remain in that condition. For the third of six times in 1 Thessalonians, the term "gospel" appears. Persuasively the apostle defends the character of himself and associates making the point that they could be entrusted with God's life-changing message, the gospel.

"Even so we speak" or *keep on speaking*, as the present tense verb indicates, "not as pleasing men." The Greek word order is as follows: "even so we are speaking not as men pleasing." In Galatians, Paul twice chooses the term "pleasing," where he pens, "For do I now persuade men, or God? Or do I seek to please men? For if I still pleased men, I would not be a bondservant of Christ" (Gal. 1:10). Rather, Paul is a God-pleaser who understands that only He "tests our hearts." Thankfully Paul, Silas, and Timothy are God-pleasers and know that only He could approve them, entrust the gospel to their care, and test their hearts.

"For neither at any time did we use flattering words, as you know, nor a cloak for covetousness—God is witness," writes Paul (v. 5). The only New Testament occurrence of "flattering" appears here in conjunction with "words," which was not the *modus operandi* of Paul, Silas, and Timothy. For the third time Paul appeals to the saints' recollection with the words "as you know" (vv. 1, 2, 5). Moreover, the holy threesome did not wear "a cloak for covetousness." Seven times the feminine noun "cloak" emerges from the Greek New Testament, which comes from the compound word meaning *before* and *to shine*, referring to an *outward show or appearance.*

Paul denies wearing a "cloak of covetousness." The NKJV translation "covetousness" literally means from the Greek *I have more,* which reveals the unchecked greediness of an individual. In Colossians Paul equates the term with idolatry (Col. 3:5). Next, he cites "God is witness," which builds upon his repetitive appeal to the witness of the Thessalonian saints (vv. 1, 2, 5, 11).

Furthermore, Paul states the following: "Nor did we seek glory from men, either from you or others." The present participle "seek" displays that the missionaries' regular practice did not consist of robbing God of the glory that belongs solely to Him. They keep their eyes fixed on Jesus and a heavenly reward, not the temporal platitudes of men!

Those who preach the gospel have the right to be sustained by the ones to whom they minister. "We might have made demands as apostles of Christ," shares Paul. After Jesus calls the twelve to Himself, He says, "for a worker is worthy of his food" (Matt. 10:10). "Apostles" surfaces only here in 1 and 2 Thessalonians. The apostle Paul apparently didn't need to use his apostolic muscle with these saints, who seem to respect his authority; however, he could have required them to care for him. For instance, in 1 Corinthians 9 the well-traveled missionary lays out six arguments why the minister is worthy of support.

"But we were gentle among you, just as a nursing mother cherishes her own children," (1 Thess. 2:7) pens the caring apostle. Paul begins with an adversative "but" showing a contrast with the previous verse. When he could have made demands based upon his apostolic authority, he declined. The adjective "gentle," which appears twice in the Greek New Testament, carries the idea *to be gentle, mild, easy, and compliant.* Second Timothy 2:24 gives us the second use, "And a servant of the Lord must not quarrel but be gentle to all."

Paul compares his ministry, along with Silas and Timothy, to that of a "nursing mother." Although "mother" appears in italics—which means it is not part of the original text but supplied by the translator for smoothness of thought—it is the right idea. "Nursing" is a *hapax legomenon* (a term only used once) and portrays the tenderness of a mother giving sustenance to her babies. The verbal form of the word means *to nourish or feed* (Matt. 6:26; 25:37; Rev. 12:6, 14). "Cherishes" likewise characterizes a caring mother who *gives warmth* to "her own children."

Loving tenderness of thought and action, not demanding behaviors, best describe Paul, Silas, and Timothy's care for the saints. "So, affectionately longing for you, we were well pleased to impart to you not only the gospel of God, but also our own lives, because you had become dear to us" (v. 8). Paul's choice of the imperfect tense verb translated "we were well pleased" shows a continual well-pleasing in the past. The thoughtful trio didn't just express a desire to share the gospel of God with the Thessalonians but also took the time "to impart" the good news to them.

Not only did the missionary team give the gospel but were willing to die for the saints at Thessalonica. "Our own soul" denotes the depth of sacrifice these committed disciples offer. "Lives" derives from the word "soul" and speaks of life itself. Elsewhere Paul boasts of Epaphroditus, "because for the work of Christ he came close to death, not regarding his life [soul], to supply what was lacking in your service toward me" (Phil. 2:30). The reason for Paul, Silas, and Timothy's sacrifice is stated: "because you had become dear to us." *Beloved* is the literal meaning of "dear." We first find the adjective used of the Father speaking about the Son at His baptism, "This is My beloved Son" (Matthew 3:17). As the Father held the Son dear, Paul, Silas, and Timothy treasure the beloved souls of the saints they serve!

Paul gives a confirmation of the affection he and his associates have toward the Thessalonians. "For you remember, brethren, our labor and toil; for laboring night and day, that we might not be a burden to any of you, we preached to you the gospel of God" (1 Thess. 2:9). Only Paul employs "labor and toil" together from the Greek New Testament (2 Cor. 11:27; 2 Thess. 3:8). "Labor" refers to a *tiresome work* (as in 1 Thess. 1:3), and "toil" being the common

46

word for labor. Toil is added to labor in the three above passages to communicate the arduous nature of the work! The strenuous effort is made "night and day," which directs the saints not to a literal working around the clock, but to the sacrificial effort he made for them!

"That we might not be a burden to any of you," imparts the purpose of the vigorous labor. "Burden" is the root meaning of the Greek term, but also has a preposition added to the term intensifying its concept. The missionaries sacrificed their own comfort, and in that context they "preached to you the gospel of God."

Again Paul appeals to the Thessalonians (vv. 1, 2, 5) and to God (v. 5) as being able to testify to these truths. He writes, "You are witnesses, and God also, how devoutly and justly and blamelessly we behaved ourselves among you who believe" (v. 10). The following three adverbs testify to the missionaries' stellar character: "devoutly," "justly," and "blamelessly." "Devoutly" occurs only here, and means *sacred* or *holy*. Its root as a noun appears in Ephesians 4:24 referring to a quality of the new (born-again) man.

"Justly," as its root suggests, means *given to justice*. Paul writes in Titus 2:11–12, "For the grace of God that brings salvation has appeared to all men, teaching us that, denying ungodliness and worldly lusts, we should live soberly, righteously [justly], and godly in the present age." The last adverb of the three is "blamelessly," and means *blamelessly* or *faultlessly*. It only comes up twice in the New Testament; the other use is found in 1 Thessalonians 5:23. Since these men of God applied the previously stated virtues, Paul could write that this is how "we behaved ourselves among you who believe."

Paul calls the church to recollect, "how we exhorted, and comforted, and charged every one of you, as a father does his own children" through the familiar words, "as you know" (vv. 1, 2, 5, 11). All three participles are given in the present tense, showing linear motion. Paul, Silas, and Timothy "exhorted" or *came alongside* these saints to encourage them. "Comfort" comes from the preposition meaning *side of* and *to speak*. The idea consists of *soothing* and *comforting through kind words*. The term appears in John 11:19 and 31 of those *comforting* Martha and Mary over the death of their brother Lazarus. "Charged" is the third participle and can be translated "testifying," as in bringing forth a witness. Paul, Silas, and Timothy solemnly charge these saints, "as a father does his own children."

The purpose of the charging is given in 1 Thessalonians 2:12. Paul writes, "that you would walk worthy of God who calls you into His own kingdom and glory." As John regularly uses the term "abide," Paul chooses the term "walk." The Thessalonian saints are to conduct themselves (the metaphorical concept of "walk") "worthy of God." Actually "worthy" is an adverb and can be translated as "worthily" just as it is used in Ephesians 4:1. "I therefore, the prisoner of the Lord, beseech you to walk worthily of the calling with which you were called." These believers have a continual summons ("calls" appears in the present tense) "into His own kingdom and glory." One article (the) governs "kingdom and glory," connecting the two closely together. Paul describes the saints' transfer from one domain to another: "He has delivered us from the power of darkness and conveyed us into the kingdom of the Son of His love" (Col. 1:13).

Hear Ye, Hear Ye, Gospel Heralds – R

"Yes, and all who desire to live godly in Christ Jesus will suffer persecution" (2 Tim. 3:12), writes the apostle Paul to Timothy shortly before being executed. Today many proclaim the prosperity gospel; it is a false message promoting health, wealth, and with an emphasis upon physical blessings. Conversely the Bible communicates a radically different message conveying a plethora of spiritual blessings coupled with physical suffering. Moreover, those who identify with Jesus and publicly live for Him will suffer persecution.

Christians have a heritage of suffering. From the commencement of time God's children have suffered, been persecuted, and in some cases experienced martyrdom. Jesus lambasts the religious leaders of His day as follows: "Therefore, indeed, I send you prophets, wise men, and scribes: some of them you will kill and crucify, and some of them you will scourge in your synagogues and persecute from city to city, that on you may come all the righteous blood shed on the earth, from the blood of righteous Abel to the blood of Zechariah, son of Berechiah, whom you murdered between the temple and the altar" (Matt. 23:34–35).

Jesus is no exception; however, He predicts His own suffering and death. "Behold, we are going up to Jerusalem," says Jesus to His followers, "and the Son of Man will be betrayed to the chief priests and to the scribes; and they will condemn Him to death and deliver Him to the Gentiles; and they will mock Him, and scourge Him, and spit on Him, and kill Him. And the third day He will rise again" (Mark 10:33–34).

Paul and Silas travel to Philippi during the apostle's second missionary journey. After expelling a demon from a "certain slave girl possessed with a spirit of divination . . . who brought her masters much profit by fortune–telling" (Acts 16:16), Paul and Silas are beaten with rods, thrown into jail, and put in stocks (Acts 16:23–24). The above experience was not uncommon for the apostle Paul and associates. Paul himself catalogs occurrences of his trials, sufferings, and persecutions demonstrating his authenticity as a missionary of Jesus Christ (2 Cor. 11:23–33).

The baton is similarly passed to the saints at Thessalonica. Paul records their suffering "having received the word in much affliction, with joy of the Holy Spirit" (1 Thess. 1:6). Throughout the ages children of the true and living God have paid a price for worshiping and serving Him. We should expect the same. Paul writes, "For to you it has been granted on behalf of Christ, not only to believe in Him, but also to suffer for His sake" (Phil. 1:29).

HEAR YE, HEAR YE, GOSPEL HERALDS – E

Jesus has called all of us to make disciples (Matt. 28:18–20). We are to do so in a way that pleases the Lord. *Proclaim the gospel with integrity despite opposition* (vv. 1–6a) is our first employment point. Paul, Silas, and Timothy herald the true gospel while maintaining lives of integrity. They carried a powerful testimony because the gospel of Jesus had transformed their lives, and all could see the evidence.

Your first assignment is to read Psalm 139. Ponder how thoroughly God knows you. Then ask the Lord to evaluate your life to see if you need to change anything, so that you can proclaim the gospel with integrity. David exclaims, "Search me, O God, and know my heart; try me, and know my anxieties; and see if there is any wicked way in me, and lead me in the way everlasting" (Psalm 139:23–24). Go and do likewise!

Proclaim the gospel gladly with self-sacrifice (1 Thess. 2:6b–9) is employment point number two. Paul, as an apostle of Jesus Christ, had every biblical right to demand the Thessalonian saints compensate him for ministry, but chose not to impose this burden on them. Your second assigned mission is to review Psalm 139:23–24, and this time ask the Lord if you are a sacrificial Christian. Jesus' demands are high; He states, "Whoever desires to come after Me, let him deny himself, and take up his cross, and follow Me" (Mark 8:34). Follow in the steps of the prophets of old, Jesus, and Paul.

Our third employment point is as follows: *Petition the saints as a godly father to kingdom living* (vv. 10–12). Go back and slowly read 1 Thessalonians 2:1–12. Notice the caring disposition of Paul and associates. Consider if you have the same fatherly and motherly nurturing characteristics. In closing consider the caring disposition of Jesus. He says, "Take My yoke upon you and learn from Me, for I am gentle and lowly in heart, and you will find rest for your souls" (Matt. 11:29).

CHAPTER FOUR

WHAT TWO THINGS SHOULD YOU WELCOME IN YOUR LIFE?

1 Thessalonians 2:13–16

A pastor is making house calls, seeking to lead people to Jesus. He reaches one home in the afternoon and rings the doorbell. He distinctively hears someone inside, but no one comes to answer the door, so after waiting a few minutes and having also knocked on the door, he takes out his business card, writes down "Revelation 3:20," and puts it on the doormat.

A few weeks later, after church service, an usher hands him the same business card, only this time, under "Revelation 3:20," there is another verse, "Genesis 3:10." Here is what each of them says: "Behold, I stand at the door and knock. If anyone hears My voice and opens the door, I will come in to him and dine with him, and he with Me." Genesis 3:10, "So he said, 'I heard Your voice in the garden, and I was afraid because I was naked; and I hid myself.'"

There are times and circumstances when it is best not to open the door and invite guests to visit. Yet we will see that there are two things that each believer should welcome into his life. Let's slowly read and digest the two passages below, which will prepare us for the F.I.R.E. to come.

For this reason we also thank God without ceasing, because when you received the word of God which you heard from us, you welcomed it not as the word of men, but as it is in truth, the word of God, which also effectively works in you who believe. For you, brethren, became imitators of the churches of God which are in Judea in Christ Jesus. For you also suffered the same things from your own countrymen, just as they did from the Judeans.

who killed both the Lord Jesus and their own prophets, and have persecuted us; and they do not please God and are contrary to all men, forbidding us to speak to the Gentiles that they may be saved, so as always to fill up the measure of their sins; but wrath has come upon them to the uttermost. (1 Thess. 2:13–16)

We always thank God that you believed the message we preached. It came from him, and it isn't something made up by humans. You accepted it as God's message, and now he is working in you. My friends, you did just like God's churches in Judea and like the other followers of Christ Jesus there. And so, you were mistreated by your own people, in the same way they were mistreated by their people.

Those [evil people] killed the Lord Jesus and the prophets, and they even chased us away. God doesn't like what they do and neither does anyone else. They keep us from speaking his message to the Gentiles and from leading them to be saved. They have always gone too far with their sins. Now God has finally become angry and will punish them. (1 Thess. 2:13–16, CEV)

WELCOMING SCRIPTURE AND SUFFERING – F

- What connection or linkage does "for this reason" make (v. 13)?
- How did the Thessalonians view "the word of God" (v. 13)?
- Whom did the Thessalonian saints imitate (v. 14)?
- What accusation does Paul make of his "own countrymen" (vv. 14b–15)?
- What does "wrath has come upon them to the uttermost" mean (v. 16)?

WELCOMING SCRIPTURE AND SUFFERING – I

"For this reason" can be translated "on account of "and connects the missionaries' entrance, suffering, and sincere care of the Thessalonians (vv. 1–12) with 1 Thessalonians 2:13–16.

Paul expresses his thankfulness, "we also thank God without ceasing, because when you received the word of God which you heard from us, you welcomed it not as the word of men, but as it is in truth, the word of God, which also effectively works in you who believe" (v. 13). The emphatic "we" expresses the gratefulness of Paul, Silas, and Timothy. "Thank" is written in the present tense, showing the linear motion of the thankfulness. Paul's practice consists of giving thanks for the saints (Rom. 1:8; 1 Cor. 1:4; Eph. 1:16–17; Phil. 1:3). Our term first appears in Matthew when Jesus "took the seven loaves and the fish and gave thanks" (Matt. 15:36). Paul imitates Jesus and then commands these saints to continue the godly tradition (1 Thess. 5:18).

"Without ceasing" derives from an adverb that first occurs in Romans 1:9, where Paul writes, "For God is my witness, whom I serve with my spirit in the gospel of His Son, that without ceasing I make mention of you always in my prayers." Paul's disciplined prayer life should be emulated. "Pray without ceasing" (1 Thess. 5:17), he later commands the saints at Thessalonica.

Willingly the saints "received the word of God" from Paul and Silas. "Received" derives from the compound verb meaning *from* and *to take*, so in essence *to take near to oneself.* These formerly lost idolaters "welcomed it not as the word of men." The Greek word "welcomed" speaks of *accepting an offer willingly and readily.* Paul uses the same term in 1 Thessalonians 1:6, "having received [welcomed] the word in much affliction, with joy of the Holy Spirit." Stated negatively, the gospel message was "not as the word of men." Then shared positively, beginning with an adversative ("but"): "as it is in truth, the word of God." "Truth" comes from an adverb occurring twenty–one times in the Greek New Testament. Its first appearance comes after Jesus calms a storm, "Truly You are the Son of God" (Matt. 14:33). As Jesus is truly God's Son, so His Word is in truth!

Inherently the Word is powerful, "which also effectively works in you who believe." The present tense verb "effectively works" reveals a continual efficient energy and also occurs here in the middle voice, which conveys an innate power to accomplish its work.

"For you, brethren, became imitators of the churches of God which are in Judea in Christ Jesus" (v. 14a). The conjunction "for" displays how effectively God's Word works. Paul addresses the brothers and sisters in Christ with an emphatic you "became imitators" or *followers* (as translated in 1 Thessalonians 1:6) of "the churches of God in Judea in Christ Jesus." Suffering believers need to be reminded occasionally that others have suffered before them as Paul does here. "Judea" might refer to Judea proper, but also could call attention to all of Israel.

Paul reminds these persecuted saints, "for you also suffered the same things from your own countrymen, just as they did from the Judeans" (v. 14b). The apostle to the Gentiles began his ministry to his fellow Jews. Yet he and fellow Jewish believers regularly suffered at the hands of their own countrymen (Acts 14:1–7, 19–20; 2 Cor. 11:24). Indeed, after such harsh treatment Paul and Barnabas turned from a targeted ministry to the Jews to focus upon the Gentiles (Acts 13:40–50). (We will probe this topic further under relationship.)

In harsh tones Paul indicts the Jews "who killed both the Lord Jesus and their own prophets, and have persecuted us; and they do not please God and are contrary to all men" (v. 15). Paul separates "Lord" from "Jesus" in the Greek text showing the gravity of the Jews' deeds. He emphasizes that they murdered the "Lord" pointing to His deity and the Man "Jesus" communicating His humanity.

The Greek text can be viewed as either connecting "the Lord Jesus and their own prophets" as victims of murder by Jews (Matt. 21:35–39) or can place "prophets" with "us," which would translate "persecuted the prophets and us" identifying Paul with the prophets. The latter view is preferred since not all the Old Testament prophets were murdered. Also, the flow seems unusual, placing Old Testament prophets after Jesus. Moreover, persecution seems to be the binding tie between Jesus, the Old Testament prophets, and Paul, Silas, and Timothy. Stephen's preaching similarly directs us to the latter view: "Which of the prophets did your fathers not persecute?" (Acts 7:52). For these reasons it seems best to identify Paul with the prophets.

Clearly the activity from Paul's own people did "not please God and are contrary to all men." The choice of "please" in the present tense tells of a continual displeasing to God. Conversely, Paul and his fellow missionaries did not seek to please men with their preaching, but God (1 Thess. 2:4). "Contrary" appears eight times from the Greek New Testament and can refer to the wind (Matt. 14:24; Mark 6:48; Acts 27:4) and Saul before he became Paul who opposed the name of Jesus (Acts 26:9). The goal of the contrary fellow countrymen: "forbidding us to speak to the Gentiles that they may be saved" (v. 16a). "Forbidding" occurs in the present tense meaning *to cut off, weaken,* and thus *to hindering* and *preventing.* John writes of Diotrephes, who loves being number one, and "forbids those who wish to [honor John through receiving missionaries], putting them out of the church" (3 John 10). The purpose of the forbidding is given, "that they may be saved."

Paul now spells out the consequences for the dastardly deeds of his fellow countrymen: "so as always to fill up the measure of their sins, but wrath has come upon them to the uttermost" (v. 16b). The expression "so as" comes from the Greek construction conveying purpose. *To fully fill up,* or *completely fill up* gives the idea behind the words "to fill up." Here the term points to measuring.

Believers will escape God's wrath (1 Thess. 1:10; 5:9) whether it is the Tribulation or eternal damnation (Rom. 5:9). Yet the unbelieving antagonist are already under God's wrath as the aorist (past tense) verb "has come" depicts. Paul articulates the future aspects of God's wrath for unbelievers in 2 Thessalonians 1:6–9.

John declares all unbelievers as currently under God's wrath and that the only means of deliverance is through Jesus Christ. He writes, "He who believes in the Son has everlasting life; and he who does not believe the Son shall not see life, but the wrath of God abides on him" (John 3:36). The full extent of God's wrath will be meted out as Paul describes "to the uttermost," which means literally *unto the end, termination,* or *completion.*

WELCOMING SCRIPTURE AND SUFFERING – R

Jesus established the order for proclaiming the gospel to the early church. After conquering death, He directs, "But you shall receive power when the Holy Spirit has come upon you; and you shall be witnesses to Me in Jerusalem, and in all Judea and Samaria, and to the end of the earth" (Acts 1:8). Clearly the Lord points the preaching of the gospel to begin with the Jews. After all, this is where Jesus started. John declares, "He came to His own, and His own did not receive Him" (John 1:11).

Saul needed a redirect; he who formerly persecuted the saints received the call of Jesus to preach the gospel. Note the order of his communication: "For I am not ashamed of the gospel of Christ, for it is the power of God to salvation for everyone who believes, for the Jew first and also for the Greek" (Rom. 1:16). Paul, formerly called Saul, embarked upon the pathway established by Jesus and commenced his ministry preaching to the Jews (Acts 9; 13:5, 14). However, the Jews repeatedly reject the gospel. Luke documents, "Then Paul and Barnabas grew bold and said, 'It was necessary that the word of God should be spoken to you [Jews] first; but since you reject it, and judge yourselves unworthy of everlasting life, behold, we turn to the Gentiles'" (Acts 13:46).

Although the apostle gives a scathing review of the Jews' rejection of the gospel (1 Thess. 2:13–16), nonetheless his love for them didn't diminish. Paul reveals the deep and abiding love for the Jewish people in the book of Romans. Emotionally he declares, "for I could wish that I myself were accursed from Christ for my brethren, my countrymen according to the flesh" (Rom. 9:3). In essence, the apostle wishes he could be accursed (as his Lord was upon the tree for the sin of the world) if God would grant him the ability to take their sins upon himself. Make no mistake, although Paul is the apostle to the Gentiles

(Rom. 11:13), his heart beats for all people to be saved, including his fellow Jews.

First Thessalonians 2:13–16 does not contradict Paul's love for the Jews, but shows a realistic assessment of their activities in the past and present concerning those whom God has sent to preach.

WELCOMING SCRIPTURE AND SUFFERING – E

Welcome the living word into your life (v. 13) is employment point number one. While under duress the Thessalonians welcomed God's Word readily. They would come to realize that the Bible will build them up spiritually (Acts 20:32), bless them spiritually (Josh. 1:8–9; Ps. 1:2–3), mature them (2 Tim. 3:16–17), give them liberty (John 8:31–32), and accomplish God's purpose (Isa. 55:11).

Your assignment is to review the above passages of Scripture. Prayerfully consider the ones that you most need currently and commit those texts to memory. As Paul said to the Ephesian elders, "so now, brethren, I commend you to God and to the word of His grace, which is able to build you up and give you an inheritance among all those who are sanctified" (Acts 20:32).

Those who have identified with the true God have suffered throughout the ages. *Welcome suffering, imitating Jesus, the prophets, and apostles* (vv. 14–16) is our second employment point. Your assignment consists of memorizing 2 Timothy 3:12, which states, "yes, and all who desire to live godly in Christ Jesus will suffer persecution." It has been said that the Christian life is not a playground but a battleground. Determine to "endure hardship as a good soldier of Jesus Christ" (2 Timothy 2:3).

Next, praise the Lord for being able to identify with all the saints throughout the ages who have suffered for their faith. Ponder Philippians 1:29, which instructs, "For to you it has been granted on behalf of Christ, not only to believe in Him, but also to suffer for His sake." The writer of Hebrews gives us the hall of faith in Hebrews 11. Then in Hebrews 12:1–2 we are reminded to keep our eyes upon Jesus, as the former saints are cheering us on to finish strong!

CHAPTER FIVE

THE DISPLAY, OPPOSITION, AND REWARD TO AUTHENTIC BELIEVERS

1 Thessalonians 2:17–20

Jones comes into the office an hour late for the third time in one week and found the boss waiting for him. "What's the story this time, Jones? Let's hear a good excuse for a change."

Jones sighed, "Everything went wrong this morning, boss. The wife decided to drive me to the station. She got ready in ten minutes, but then the drawbridge got stuck. Rather than let you down, I swam across the river—look, my suit is still damp—ran out to the airport, got a ride on Mr. Smith's helicopter, landed on top of Radio City Music Hall, and was carried piggyback by one of the employees."

The boss, who was obviously disappointed said, "Jones, you'll have to do better than that. No woman can be ready in ten minutes."

Jones clearly made quite an effort (or at least developed quite a story) to get to work. The apostle Paul also struggled to return to see the beloved Thessalonian saints. His effort, although opposed by the devil, revealed a great care for these believers.

Before perusing the Bible, let's consider the following three questions. How can you show Jesus' love to believers? Also, what should you expect in the process? Finally, how will you be rewarded in the present and future?

But we, brethren, having been taken away from you for a short time in presence, not in heart, endeavored more eagerly to see your face with great desire. Therefore we wanted to come to you—even I, Paul, time and again—but Satan hindered us. For what is our hope, or joy, or crown of rejoicing? Is it not even you in the presence of our Lord Jesus Christ at His coming? For you are our glory and joy. (1 Thess. 2:17–20)

But we, brethren, having been taken away from you for a short while—in person, not in spirit—were all the more eager with great desire to see your face. For we wanted to come to you—I, Paul, more than once—and yet Satan hindered us. For who is our hope or joy or crown of exultation? Is it not even you, in the presence of our Lord Jesus at His coming? For you are our glory and joy. (1 Thess. 2:17–20, NASB)

STRIVING TOWARD THE CROWN OF REJOICING – F

- What role does "but we" play in our former and current passage (v. 17)?

- What might have led Paul to choose these words to pen (v. 17)?

- Who kept Paul and Silas from returning to Thessalonica (v. 18)?

- Is it unusual for Paul to sign his name in the middle of an epistle (v. 18)?

- When will the faithful believer receive the "crown of rejoicing" (v. 19)?

- Do you have a similar view as Paul did toward those you serve (v. 20)?

STRIVING TOWARD THE CROWN OF REJOICING – I

Paul begins the new paragraph with the words "but we." The former is an adversative showing a sharp contrast by Paul, Silas, and Timothy with the hate-filled Jews (vv. 14b–16) and the emphatic "we" strengthens the distinction. Affectionately Paul once again addresses the saints as "brethren." Spiritually they are *from the same womb* through the blood of Jesus Christ.

The loving spiritual father continues, "having been taken away from you for a short time in presence, not in heart, endeavored more eagerly to see your face with great desire" (v. 17). "Having been taken away" derives from a compound term literally meaning "from an orphan," which communicates *having been orphaned*. Paul's affectionate tone starkly contrasts how those who drove him out of Thessalonica most likely accused him of not caring for them since he hasn't returned. The passive voice of "having been orphaned" testifies that the severing from them was not his choice.

The expression "for a short time in presence, not in heart" shows that out of sight is not out of mind. It was a short *season*, which is the concept of "time." Paul shows a deep and abiding intimacy with these saints through the words "in presence." As Moses longs to see the face of God (Ex. 33:18–20), Paul longs to be *toward the face* or *eyes* of the Thessalonians, which is the denotation of "presence." In other words, he longs to be up close and personal with his spiritual children. "Not in heart" presents the pain Paul and Silas experience having been separated from their spiritual offspring.

"Endeavored," in the expression "endeavored more eagerly to see your face with desire" carries the sense of *diligence* and *earnestness*. It is translated "be diligent" in 2 Timothy 4:9 when Paul senses the end is coming, and commands Timothy, "be diligent to come to me quickly." In the same epistle Paul again commands Timothy, "Do your utmost [be diligent] to come before winter" (2 Tim. 4:21). "More eagerly," which is an adverb of comparative degree, intensifies how determined Paul was to return and visit these saints.

Paul names the cause of his inability to get back to Thessalonica. "Therefore we wanted to come to you—even I, Paul, time and again—but Satan hindered us" (1 Thess. 2:18). The apostle's wish ("we wanted") here points not only to a desire of the will but toward his strong feelings, which emotional appeal shines brightly through our passage. Suddenly, and perhaps unexpectedly, Paul changes from first person plural ("we") to the first person singular ("I"). Then he uses his name in the middle of the epistle as a personal appeal. Elsewhere he does the same thing in a few places. Second Corinthians 10:1 gives the following: "Now I, Paul, myself am pleading with you." Then in Galatians 5:2, "Indeed I, Paul say to you" and also Ephesians 3:1, "For this reason, I, Paul, the prisoner of Christ Jesus for you Gentiles."

Great effort had been made to circle back to see the saints at Thessalonica. "Time and again" literally translated is "once and twice," yet that expression can also be used to indicate several times. Believers have a great *adversary*, which is the meaning of the name "Satan," who opposed Paul and Silas from returning to see the saints. (Satan's activity in hindering children of God will be more fully investigated under relationship.)

"Hindered" derives from a compound term composed from the preposition *in* and the verb *to cut down* or *strike*. The metaphorical use as given in our passage conveys *to hinder* or *impede*. In secular language the term refers to breaking up a road to prevent an enemy's advance. It should be observed that the wicked one does not cause all hindrances (Rom. 15:22; Acts 16:6–7). Yet Paul had enough discernment to know that Satan did the hindering in this situation.

Paul asks the following thoughtful questions: "For what is our hope, or joy, or crown of rejoicing? Is it not even you in the presence of our Lord Jesus Christ at His coming?" (v. 19). He begins with "our hope" that speaks about a future expectation based upon historical truth. Concerning the Rapture, Paul writes, "But I do not want you to be ignorant, brethren, concerning those who have fallen asleep, lest you sorrow as others who have no hope" (1 Thess. 4:13). He then argues that the saints' hope is based upon the Lord's death and resurrection (historical truths). "For if [the first-class condition assumes the statement to be true] we believe that Jesus died and rose again, even so God will bring with Him those who sleep in Jesus" (1 Thess. 4:14).

The feminine noun "joy" derives from the fruit of the Spirit (Gal. 5:22). Circumstances don't control the gladness children of God experience, since the Spirit of the living God produces this fruit. Next, "crown of rejoicing" could be translated a "crown, which is boasting" and aims toward the Rapture when Jesus praises believers. This is not a literal crown, but the "crown of rejoicing" appears metaphorically of the time the believer is perfected with complete glory and commended by their Lord.

Paul abruptly interrupts his first question and interjects a second question expecting the answer yes. "Is it not even you in the presence of our Lord Jesus Christ at His coming?" The apostle envisions the day when these spiritual children are ushered into Jesus' "presence." This term is made up of two prepositions ("in" and "before") and a suffix denoting direction. They will stand before "our Lord Jesus Christ." While "Lord" refers to Jesus' deity, His name (Jesus) points to His humanity, and "Christ" to Him being the *Messiah*, or *Anointed One*. "Coming," which conveys *to be present*, is a technical term used of the Rapture (John 2:28) and Second Coming (Matt. 24:3). Here it is used of the Rapture, as in 1 Thessalonians 4:15.

Beautifully the apostle pens, "For you are our glory and joy" (v. 20). Paul addresses the saints with an emphatic "you," which should also shut the mouths of the apostle's critics; he loves the Thessalonian saints very much. "You are" communicates that presently (now) these saints are Paul's glory and joy, whereas 1 Thessalonians 2:19 shows this to also be true in the future.

It is time again to consider the broader implications of this passage.

STRIVING TOWARD THE CROWN OF REJOICING – R

Discernment is a hallmark with Paul. He perceives that "Satan hindered us" (1 Thess. 2:18) from the multiple planned trips to Thessalonica. In today's vernacular, the devil blew up the road so that Paul and Silas could not return to encourage the saints. Since the beginning in the garden of Eden Satan has sought to hinder both Old and New Testament saints in their lives and ministry. We will investigate various ways the devil plies his trade.

Satan masterfully seeks to tempt all believers. He even attempts to do the same to Jesus. Matthew records, "Now when the tempter came to Him, he said, 'If you are the Son of God, command that these stones become bread'" (Matt. 4:3). Both Matthew and Luke (Luke 4) document Satan's temptations of Jesus using the lust of the flesh, the lust of the eyes, and the pride of life. The apostle John warns believers of the world's system, consisting of "the lust of the flesh, the lust of the eyes, and the pride of life" (1 John 2:16). The serpent of old used these tactics on Adam and Eve (Gen. 3) and Jesus (Matt. 4; Luke 4), and uses them today upon believers.

The prince of darkness gets credit for keeping spiritual blinders on the unsaved. Paul is aware of his devices (2 Cor. 2:11) instructing, "But even if our gospel is veiled, it is veiled to those who are perishing, whose minds the god of this age has blinded" (2 Cor. 4:3-4). Believers need to thank God, "for it is the God who commanded light to shine out of darkness, who has shone in our hearts to give the light of the knowledge of the glory of God in the face of Jesus Christ" (2 Cor. 4:6). Praise be to the God of light!

Deception is another tool of Satan. Truly he is a master deceiver and recognized as such in the Bible (see Rev. 12:9). Paul exposes the manipulator as follows: "But I fear, lest somehow, as the serpent deceived Eve by his craftiness, so your minds may be corrupted from the simplicity that is in Christ" (2 Cor. 11:3). The Greek term for "deceived" has an intensifier prefixed to the verb, which shows the strength of Satan's deceptions.

Not only does the devil blind the eyes of the lost, but also wields influence upon the saints when he finds a willing participant. Clearly he saw an open door (or heart) with Ananias and Sapphira (Acts 5:1–11), which led to their demise. Peter, before pronouncing sentence on Ananias asks, "why has Satan filled your heart to lie to the Holy Spirit and keep back part of the price of the land for yourself?" (Acts 5:3). Be advised, dear child of God, that Satan is no friend to Old and New Testament saints and desires to influence you negatively also.

Ready to go to work? Good! Let's put on our work clothes as we transition to employment.

STRIVING TOWARD THE CROWN OF REJOICING – E

Display authentic Christianity by planning time with believers (v. 17) gives us our first employment point. God is detail-oriented; His plans reflect an orderly nature. Throughout the Bible the Lord stresses the importance of His people to worship and serve Him. Only two chapters in the Bible describe creation (Genesis 1 and 2). Yet there are a plethora of chapters on the structure of the tabernacle, responsibilities of the priests, as well as the responsibilities of the people (Ex. 25–40). So, in order to spend time with people, there should be commensurate planning. Jesus commanded us "to make disciples of all the nations" (Matt. 28:19), and Paul governs Timothy about choosing the right men for training (2 Tim. 2:1–2). Likewise, we should structure our lives and schedules to meet with believers for fellowship, discipleship, and serving God's people. Consider your schedule and make necessary changes in order to *display authentic Christianity by planning time with believers.*

We have seen how Satan thwarted Paul and Timothy from returning to Thessalonica. *Expect Satanic opposition when attempting to serve believers* (v. 18) is our second employment point. Christians must put on the full armor of God, with the realization that we are engaged in a battle (Eph. 6:11–20). The warfare consists of attacks from an unseen enemy (Eph. 6:12). Therefore, our mindset should prepare us for battle. Paul reminds Timothy, "You therefore must endure hardship as a good soldier of Jesus Christ" (2 Tim. 2:3). Again, the Christian life is a battleground and not a playground. God's children should not be surprised from the attacks from the enemy, but anticipate them by being fully clad with the Lord's protective gear!

Experience present and future joy for serving believers (vv. 19-20) is our third employment point. Jesus is recorded as saying, "it is more blessed to give than to receive" (Acts 20:35). Paul enjoys joy unspeakable for his investment in the saints. Serving them is not only a pleasure in this life, but will lead to a future reward with eternal benefits. "Therefore, my beloved brethren," exhorts Paul to the Corinthians, "be steadfast, immovable, always abounding in the work of the Lord, knowing that your labor is not in vain in the Lord" (1 Cor. 15:58).

Chapter Six

Sacrificing Your Security for Others Shows What?

1 Thessalonians 3:1–5

Three soldiers invade enemy territory by order of the commander. Shortly after setting up their camp, notification of two other important missions via radio communication is relayed. The veteran sergeant understands the gravity of the pressing needs and makes a decision. He chooses to remain in hostile terrain, and sacrificially dispatches his well-trained two soldiers to the other hot spots while remaining alone.

Paul finds himself in a similar situation. He travels to Athens and subsequently commands Silas and Timothy to join him (Acts 17:15). Apparently after joining the veteran apostle in Athens Silas leaves Paul for another assignment while Timothy is sent to check on the status of the Thessalonian saints (1 Thess. 3:1–2). Sacrificially, Paul remains alone in the philosophical capital of the world.

There are three questions for your consideration I'd like you to briefly consider before turning to our two translations of the text. Like the veteran sergeant and Paul, would you sacrifice your security for others? Also, have you trained soldiers of Christ for difficult assignments? Finally, how well do you know the spiritual status of your disciples?

Therefore, when we could no longer endure it, we thought it good to be left in Athens alone, and sent Timothy, our brother and minister of God, and our fellow laborer in the gospel of Christ, to establish you and encourage you concerning your faith, that no one should be shaken by these afflictions; for you yourselves know that we are appointed to this. For, in fact, we told you before when we were with you that we would suffer tribulation, just as it happened, and you know. For this reason, when I could no longer endure it, I sent to know your faith, lest by some means the tempter had tempted you, and our labor might be in vain. (1 Thess. 3:1–5)

So when we could stand it no longer, we thought it best to be left by ourselves in Athens. We sent Timothy, who is our brother and co-worker in God's service in spreading the gospel of Christ, to strengthen and encourage you in your faith, so that no one would be unsettled by these trials. For you know quite well that we are destined for them. In fact, when we were with you, we kept telling you that we would be persecuted. And it turned out that way, as you well know. For this reason, when I could stand it no longer, I sent to find out about your faith. I was afraid that in some way the tempter had tempted you and that our labors might have been in vain. (1 Thess. 3:1–5, NIV)

SAINTLY SACRIFICES TO STABILIZE THE SAINTS – F

- What is the "therefore" there for in 1 Thessalonians 3:1?
- Why does Paul choose to be an orphan (v. 1)?
- How does Paul know he can trust Timothy for this mission (v. 2)?
- Who is appointed to suffer for Jesus (v. 3)?
- What model of suffering does Paul place before the Thessalonians (v. 4)?
- Where is Paul concerned that temptation comes from (v. 5)?

SAINTLY SACRIFICES TO STABILIZE THE SAINTS – I

The "therefore" in "Therefore, when we could no longer endure it, we thought it good to be left in Athens alone" (v. 1) connects the previous section of Paul attempting to visit (2:17–20) to why he then dispatches Timothy. "Endure" literally means *to cover*, but Paul does not seek to conceal his emotions or feelings toward his spiritual children; it is just the opposite. Paul could not *hold out* any longer, which is the metaphorical use of "endure." He had to know their condition!

Although Paul writes "we thought it good to be left in Athens alone," he refers to only himself. It seems the apostle is allergic to drawing self-attention. Paul arrives in Athens without Timothy and Silas (Acts 17:14), and later they join him (Acts 17:15). Subsequently Paul sends Timothy again to Thessalonica (1 Thess. 3:5). Note the "I" and not "we" in 1 Thessalonians 3:5, "For this reason, when I could no longer endure it, I sent to know your faith." Most likely Paul dispatched Silas elsewhere. (His argument is undermined if Silas is with him.)

Paul's terminology "to be left" reveals the depth of his sacrifice. The infinitive carries an intensifier (preposition) and means *to leave behind* and is found in secular language of leaving someone you love at death; it carries the idea of feeling *abandoned* or *forsaken*. One of the twenty-five New Testament uses arises in Luke. Jesus asks, "What man of you, having a hundred sheep, if he loses one of them, does not leave [abandon] the ninety-nine in the wilderness, and go after the one which is lost until he finds it?" (Luke 15:4). Graciously and sacrificially Paul willingly felt like an abandoned orphan at Athens (by choice), in order to care for the saints at Thessalonica.

His selfless action is described, "and sent Timothy, our brother and minister of God, and our fellow laborer in the gospel of Christ, to establish you and encourage you concerning your faith" (v. 2). An executive decision is made by Paul *to send* or *dispatch*—which is the concept of "sent"—his son in the faith to Thessalonica. The verb "sent" can be used of an official capacity as in John the Baptist, who "sent two of his disciples" (Matt. 11:2) to learn about Jesus.

Timothy, whose name derives from *value* or *honor* and *God,* receives high praise from Paul and others. The first of twenty-four New Testament references to Timothy materializes in Acts 16:1, "Then he [Paul] came to Derbe and Lystra. And behold, a certain disciple was there, named Timothy. The son of a certain Jewish woman who believed, but his father was Greek." Luke continues, "He was well spoken of by the brethren who were at Lystra and Iconium" (Acts 16:2). Paul could send Timothy whom he calls "my beloved and faithful son" (1 Cor. 4:17) knowing the depth of his character (see Phil. 2:19–23).

Further Paul describes Timothy as "our brother and minister of God." The term "minister" first surfaces from the Greek New Testament in Matthew 20:26. Jesus says, "but whoever desires to become great among you, let him be your servant." Originally the word spoke of waiters (John 2:5, 9), pointing to lowly servants. Moreover, Paul says that Timothy is "our fellow laborer in the gospel of Christ." In the New Testament the term "fellow laborer" only appears of laborers and helpers in Christian service. Priscilla and Aquila are first designated by the term "who risked their own necks for my life" (Rom. 16:4), writes Paul. Epaphroditus similarly almost died doing ministry (Phil. 2:26–27).

Timothy partnered with Paul "in the gospel of Christ." If the expression "of Christ" is a subjective genitive, then the meaning is the gospel, which is Christ's, and He commissions it to be preached. Perhaps the objective genitive gives us the original concept, which conveys the gospel that tells us about Christ. After all, Jesus is the focus of Paul and Timothy's preaching (1 Cor. 2:1–5; 15:3–4). Paul's purpose for dispatching Timothy is as follows: "to establish you and encourage you concerning your faith." *To buttress* or *support* imparts the original meaning of "to establish." It is a key term in this chapter (3:13); we will see it again in 2 Thessalonians 2:17 and 3:3.

Moreover, the definite article ("the") links two infinitives: establish and encourage. The latter term comes into view from the Greek New Testament 108 times and refers to *coming alongside of to give support*. Paul initially encouraged the saints at Thessalonica (2:11, where the verb is translated "exhorted"), and the faith of these saints then encouraged Paul, Silas, and Timothy (3:7). Speaking of the faith of the Thessalonians, it is prevalent (3:2, 5, 6, 7, 10). Our passage (3:2) emphasizes the continuing of their faith as in Colossians 1:23, "if indeed you continue in the faith." God has a purpose in testing the faith of these saints. James instructs, "Knowing that the testing of your faith produces patience" (James 1:3).

Paul had just addressed the primary sending of Timothy to the saints (v. 2). Now he gives the secondary purpose, "that no one should be shaken by these afflictions; for you yourselves know that we are appointed to this" (v. 4). If the believers at Thessalonica are established through Timothy's encouragement, then the saints won't be moved. "Be shaken" originally referred to a dog's wagging tail—to get attention—and subsequently *to flatter*. The figurative idea before us communicates *to disturb the mind*. Timothy's encouragement should lead to the saints not being disturbed in mind "by these afflictions." Earlier Paul explains how the saints "received the word in much affliction" (1 Thess. 1:6).

Once again Paul appeals to the Thessalonians' knowledge: "for you yourselves know that we are appointed to this." The apostle's terminology "for your yourselves know" is emphatic from the Greek. He began pointing them back to their complete knowledge in the first two chapters (1:4, 5; 2:1, 2, 5, 11) and continues doing the same (3:3, 4). "We are appointed to this" can have the narrow use of "we" pointing to Paul, Silas, and Timothy. For instance in Acts 9:16, the Lord says to Ananias about Paul, "For I will show him how many things he must suffer for My name's sake." Yet the broader view of "we" seems preferable, since both the missionary team and Thessalonian saints endured persecution. Barnabas and Paul exhort the saints in

Acts 14:22, "We must through many tribulations enter the kingdom of God." Jesus stresses the same thing (John 16:33).

"For, in fact," stresses Paul, "we told you before when we were with you that we would suffer tribulation" (v. 4). Wisely, the apostle had previously prepared his recent converts by informing them that suffering can be expected by those who identify with Jesus. Paul maintains this posture to the end: "Yes, and all who desire to live godly in Christ Jesus will suffer persecution" (2 Tim. 3:12).

How did Paul endure great opposition since the inception of his ministry? He opines, "For I consider that the sufferings of this present time are not worthy to be compared with the glory which shall be revealed in us" (Rom. 8:18). "Just as it happened, and you know" became the experience for both these emissaries of God and the Thessalonians (Acts 17:5–10).

Paul closes our section with the same introductory formula he used in 1 Thessalonians 2:13: "For this reason, when I could no longer endure it, I sent to know your faith, lest by some means the tempter had tempted you, and our labor might be in vain" (v. 5). The translation "for this reason" refers to the previous verse and the predicted and confirmed suffering. Strategically the apostle moves from the first-person plural "we" in 1 Thessalonians 3:1 to the first-person singular "I" with the wording, "when I could no longer endure it." This was personal to Paul!

He again uses the first person singular, "I sent to know your faith." Earlier Paul expresses the team's care for these saints (vv. 1–2) and now his own personal feeling. Referring to "the tempter" points to Satan. The first two uses of the verb are used of the devil (Matt. 4:1, 3) in his temptations of Jesus. Actually the term is neutral, which means the desire can be good (Matt. 22:35; John 6:6; Rev. 2:2) or bad (James 1:13–14). It is used in the latter sense of Ananias and Sapphira "to test the Spirit of the Lord" (Acts 5:9). Paul didn't want the missionary effort to "be in vain," meaning *to be empty* or *hollow* (Gal. 2:2; Phil. 2:16; 1 Thess. 2:1). In essence, the trio didn't want their labor to be without success or fruitless.

We now have a better understanding of the immediate context of our passage. Let's broaden our comprehension under relationship.

SAINTLY SACRIFICES TO STABILIZE THE SAINTS – R

Security is a basic need to humanity; all of us deeply desire to know we are safe and sound. Yet Paul willingly gave up the comfort of having a ministry partner in order to extend his ministry reach. Where did he derive the vision to give up his own life for the sake of others? Moreover, where does he develop such a courageous spirit? We will now consider these thought-provoking questions.

The apostle makes the difficult decision to dispatch both Silas and Timothy to other ministry spots, which left him all alone. God uses Paul's willingness to be like an orphan because it reminds the Thessalonian saints how much he loves them. Jesus had told Paul concerning his thorn in the flesh, "My grace is sufficient for you, for My strength is made perfect in weakness" (2 Cor. 12:9). No wonder Paul adds, "Therefore most gladly I will rather boast in my infirmities, that the power of Christ may rest upon me." Paul's active application to be positionally co-crucified (denying self) with Christ (Gal. 2:20) bears fruit at Thessalonica.

Jesus becomes the model to Paul and all subsequent followers to imitate when it comes to self-sacrifice. The apostle understands this concerning Christ's emptying out of self for the sake of others (Phil. 2:6–9). This is why Paul commands the Philippians saints, "Let this mind be in you which was also in Christ Jesus" (Phil. 2:5). Paul documents the Lord's willingness to be alone in order to care for others and then gives notable examples of those who follow His lead in Philippians 2.

Tracing the Lord's footsteps, Paul declares, "Yes, and if I am being poured out as a drink offering on the sacrifice and service of your faith, I am glad and rejoice with you all" (Phil. 2:17). While under house arrest the apostle thinks he might die for his faith, and rejoices as one who imitates his Lord. Next, Timothy is cited as a "like-minded" (literally "like-souled") brother who cares for others at his own expense (Phil. 2:19–23). Finally, Paul shares the story of Epaphroditus, who nearly died in his service for others (Phil. 2:25–30).

Jesus led the example for us to follow, and then personally gives us the grace to do so courageously. Let's derive our security from the One who promises to remain with us until He calls us home!

SAINTLY SACRIFICES TO STABILIZE THE SAINTS – E

Sacrifice your security for the saints' security (v. 1) relays our first employment point and builds upon what we just studied. There are times that the Christian pilgrimage gets lonely when in service for our King. Yet we must determine to not only trace the steps of Jesus but also walk in them. Greatness doesn't come from how many people serve us. Rather, it derives from becoming the slave of all. Jesus says, and I want you to meditate upon this, "but whoever desires to become great among you shall be your servant" (Mark 10:43).

Our second employment point is conferred upon us from 1 Thessalonians 3:2–4: *Send well-trained servants to stabilize the saints.* Thankfully Paul had invested in Silas and Timothy to prepare them for their assigned tasks. Timothy would actually remind the Thessalonians of Paul's ways and practices. Paul writes, "For this reason I have sent Timothy to you, who is my beloved and faithful son in the Lord, who will remind you of my ways in Christ, as I teach everywhere in every church" (1 Cor. 4:17). Your assignment is to prayerfully seek God to show you those you are meant to train, and then in obedience fulfill the Great Commission.

Seek to know the saints' spiritual status is the third employment point (v. 5). You must be part investigator to do the work of ministry. When the Lord has granted you the privilege to train others, you must regularly seek to know how they are doing spiritually. Make a plan to systematically check on those whom the Lord has entrusted to your care. Jesus regularly took His disciples aside to know how they were doing. Wisdom decrees you do the same!

CHAPTER SEVEN

BE GOOD NEWS TO ENERGIZE
YOUR SPIRITUAL LEADERS

1 Thessalonians 3:6–10

As cold water to a weary soul, so is good news from a far country. (Prov. 25:25)

God has graced our church's ministry on the border of Washington, DC to serve people in distant locations. We have hundreds of sermons uploaded to YouTube. Outside of the United States, the most viewed sermons are in the Philippines and India. (Currently we have gleaned a missionary in both the Philippines and India through our outreach.)

I have cultivated precious friendships in these distant lands. The Lord has extended my discipleship ministry more than eight thousand miles. These dear people have trusted me to help shepherd their souls. Yet at times we have been cut off via communication because of internet interruptions due to inclement weather; however, when the power is restored and communication flows freely, and I learn that they are spiritually and physically fine, I feel reinvigorated.

Paul had been separated from the Thessalonians on account of persecution (Acts 17). Subsequently, he dispatched Timothy to learn of their spiritual status. So, let's consider two questions before prayerfully reading our texts: How can you energize your spiritual leaders? Also, what steps can you take to stabilize your disciples?

But now that Timothy has come to us from you, and brought us good news of your faith and love, and that you always have good remembrance of us, greatly desiring to see us, as we also to see you—therefore, brethren, in all our affliction and distress we were comforted concerning you by your faith. For now we live, if you stand fast in the Lord.

For what thanks can we render to God for you, for all the joy with which we rejoice for your sake before our God, night and day praying exceedingly that we may see your face and perfect what is lacking in your faith? (1 Thess. 3:6–10)

Timothy has come back from his visit with you and has told us about your faith and love. He also said that you always have happy memories of us and that you want to see us as much as we want to see you.

My friends, even though we have a lot of trouble and suffering, your faith makes us feel better about you. Your strong faith in the Lord is like a breath of new life. How can we possibly thank God enough for all the happiness you have brought us? Day and night we sincerely pray that we will see you again and help you to have an even stronger faith. (1 Thess. 3:6–10, CEV)

TIMOTHY'S REPORT AND PAUL'S RESPONSE – F

- How does Paul use the conjunction "but" in 1 Thessalonians 3:6?
- What did Timothy's "good news" reveal (v. 6)?
- How did Timothy's "good news" impact Paul, Silas, and Timothy (vv. 7–8)?
- Why does Paul offer thanksgiving (v. 9)?
- What were Paul's aspirations for the saints at Thessalonica (v. 10)?

TIMOTHY'S REPORT AND PAUL'S RESPONSE – I

The apostle Paul begins the paragraph with a contrasting opening word. "But now that Timothy has come to us from you, and brought us good news of your faith and love, and that you always have good remembrance of us, greatly desiring to see us, as we also to see you" (v. 6). "But" gives a contrast, moving from the past (2:1–3:5) and Paul's struggle (3:1–5) to the present (3:6–10). "Now" grants an adverb of time meaning *at this moment* and occurs in the emphatic position. We are not sure how long Timothy had been gone, but Paul's account in 1 Thessalonians 3:6 aligns with his arrival in Corinth (Acts 18:5) where Paul had remained (Acts 18:1).

Timothy is the vessel of good news. The verb "brought good news" appears fifty-five times in the Greek New Testament from the compound term meaning *to proclaim good news*. Fifty-four uses pertain to sharing the gospel or good tidings about the kingdom. Paul could have chosen another word, but considers Timothy's good news about the Thessalonian saints of utmost importance. The younger associate of Paul heralded good news of the saints' "faith and love." Both terms have a definite article ("the"), giving them specificity and distinction, but also encapsulating their Christian lives just as Paul writes to the Galatians: "faith working through love" (Gal. 5:6). "Faith" is a recurring theme in this chapter (vv. 2, 5), and "love" speaks of their will focused upon serving God and finding their satisfaction in Him (1 Thess. 1:3).

Thankfully the saints at Thessalonica "always have [a] good remembrance of us," writes Paul. "Have" is a present tense verb showing linear motion and "good" tells of these believers' recollection of the influence and benevolence of Paul, Silas, and Timothy. The noun "remembrance" emerges seven times from the Greek New Testament, conveying *recollection* or *remembrance* as in Philippians 1:3 where Paul pens, "I thank my God upon every remembrance of you." Paul affixes an intensifier (preposition) to the present participle "greatly desiring," which speaks of an *earnest desire*. Its first use comes from Romans

1:11: "For I long [greatly desiring] to see you, that I may impart to you some spiritual gift." Years later Paul would share with Timothy, "greatly desiring to see you, being mindful of your tears, that I may be filled with joy" (2 Tim. 1:4). The apostle confirms that the yearning is mutual, "as we also to see you."

"Therefore, brethren," writes Paul, "in all our affliction and distress we were comforted concerning you by your faith" (v. 7). *For this reason* or *on account of this* explains the two Greek words translated "therefore." Here Paul uses the singular rationale ("for this reason"), expressing how Timothy's report brought consolation to the suffering missionaries. "Brethren" reminds the saints that the blood of Jesus made them family. Good news helps heal the "affliction," which communicates *pressure* or *to be squeezed* (as used in 1 Thessalonians 1:6 and 3:3), and "distress," which conveys *necessity* or *a compelling force* (the opposite of willingness). One article governs the two terms showing two facets of a similar circumstance.

"We were comforted" is the result of the wonderful message Timothy shared with Paul. Commentators and translators are split whether to translate the verb as "comforted" or "encouraged." Perhaps both concepts are derived from the Greek term, with the latter being more prevalent. The idea of encouragement carries into 1 Thessalonians 3:8. Yet the comfort and encouragement came "by your faith." Again the Thessalonian saints' faith is of prime importance to Paul, as the term appears for the fourth time in this chapter (vv. 2, 5, 6, 7).

"For now we live, if you stand fast in the Lord," continues Paul (v. 8). The "for" gives the reason why Paul thrived and not just survived. "Now" is the adverb of time, revealing *at the present time*. Both facets *to live* and *thrive* come from "we live." From the Greek translation of the Old Testament (LXX), the exclamation conveys both aspects of "we live" to Saul as the leader of the nation: "Long live the king" (1 Sam. 10:24). The "you" in the conditional statement "if you stand" is emphatic, and the present tense verb "stand fast" shows a *continually fixed standing.* Elsewhere it refers to standing fixed in the faith (Phil. 1:27; 4:1). Paul employs the term in 1 Corinthians 16:13: "Watch, stand fast in the faith, be brave, be strong." The apostle, Silas, and Timothy immediately live and thrive when the Thessalonians are regularly standing firm "in the Lord."

"For what thanks can we render to God for you," expresses Paul, "for all the joy with which we rejoice for your sake before our God" (v. 9). "For" connects with the previous section and elaborates upon Paul's newfound energy from the good report. The noun "thanks" has its origin from the prefix *good* or *well* and *to give* or *grant*, which therefore shows gratitude or thanksgiving, whereas "we render" arises from three words (two prepositions and one verb). *In place of* or *in exchange of* begins the term followed by the second preposition *from* and then the verb *to give*. Stated negatively, it means *to repay with evil* or *avenge* (Rom. 12:19; 2 Thess. 1:6), yet asserted positively connotes *to give what is good*, as in Luke 14:14 to those who have cared for the outcasts and downtrodden in society, "And you will be blessed, because they cannot repay you; for you shall be repaid at the resurrection of the just."

The rendering of thanksgiving is "to God for you." Ten times in 1 Thessalonians 3:6–10 the word "you" or "your" surfaces, which manifests Paul's focus! Paul's reason and expression of thanksgiving is "for all the joy with which we rejoice for your sake before our God." The saints should practice rejoicing continually whether in good times or suffering during bad circumstances. Paul commands continual rejoicing (1 Thess. 5:16), and both the saints at Thessalonica (1:6) and Paul did exactly that (1 Thess. 3:9).

The following shows the fervent prayer from the missionary team for the Thessalonian saints: "night and day praying exceedingly that we may see your face and perfect what is lacking in your faith?" (v. 10). "Night and day" does not designate two set times to pray, but speaks of continual prayers (1 Thess. 5:17). Paul uses the normal term for "praying" found twenty-two times from the Greek New Testament, which means *to ask, beg,* or *express one's need.* Luke uses the term of Jesus who intercedes for Peter, "But I have prayed for you ["you" is singular and refers specifically to Peter] that your faith should not fail;

and when you have returned to Me, strengthen the brethren" (Luke 22:32). *Over and above* transmits the meaning of "exceedingly," showing that the pastoral staff exceeded all bounds and abundantly above measure prayed for the saints.

"That we may see your face and perfect what is lacking in your faith," relays Paul's purposeful prayer. Regardless of the maniacal misrepresentation that happened behind the back of this godly trio accusing them of not caring for the saints, they truly longed to *behold their face* or *the eyes*, which is the meaning of the "face." Paul expresses the same sentiment in 1 Thessalonians 2:17. The discerning threesome, having shepherds' hearts, want to "perfect" the saints. In other words, they want to positively adjust their spiritual condition, helping them to mature. Although the church is a model for others (1:7), Paul desires to supply "what is lacking in your faith." *To fall behind* furnishes the meaning of "lacking." God's children need to progress in their faith regardless of their level of maturity (1 Thess. 4:9–10).

TIMOTHY'S REPORT AND PAUL'S RESPONSE – R

Each person on planet Earth inherits a selfish nature from Adam (Ps. 51:5), and for this reason naturally focuses upon self. God's Holy Spirit, knowing the depth of self in each person, guides Paul to pen, "Let nothing be done through selfish ambition or conceit, but in lowliness of mind let each esteem others better than himself. Let each of you look out not only for his own interests, but also for the interests of others" (Phil. 2:3–4). Thankfully the mature apostle overcomes the natural inclination to self, and ten separate times writes "you" or "your" to the Thessalonian saints in 1 Thessalonians 3:6–10. You might call Paul's disease "otherism"; this made-up term also describes how we need to be diagnosed with this infectious Christian "malady."

Otherism permeates the epistle to the Thessalonians. Repeatedly the apostle appeals to the recollection of these saints to remember how the missionary triad selflessly served them (2:1, 2, 5, 11). Not only that, Paul endured isolation in pagan Athens to meet the needs of others (3:1). Paul, Silas, and Timothy had no need for the bright lights of the stage. Rather, with a spirit of unity they sacrificially give of themselves even to the point of their own demise (2:8). Instead of using their authority and receiving compensation for the ministry, they choose to work in secular employment, so not to burden the Thessalonian saints (2:9). Moreover, they display moral integrity by not seeking anything improper from the saints, but instead exhorting them to live in light of God's kingdom (2:10–11).

As Jesus laid down His life for us, we must do the same for others. Thankfully we have the godly examples of Paul, Silas, and Timothy before us. We should marvel how Paul struggles to use the word "I." He would rather refer to Timothy and Silas instead of drawing attention to self. May God help us to use "you" and "your" in our speech. and let our actions testify that we have caught the wonderful Christian disease known as otherism!

TIMOTHY'S REPORT AND PAUL'S RESPONSE – E

The breadth and depth of God's Word should cause us to be amazed. Just in one passage we will see how to encourage our spiritual leaders and the need to help our disciples become mature in the faith. *Energize your spiritual leaders by remaining steadfast in the faith* (vv. 6–8) is our first employment point. Pastors, missionaries, and church planters receive a healthy dose of revitalization when those that they have led to the Lord and disciple remain fixed in the faith. That's why Paul writes, "For now we live, if you stand fast in the Lord" (3:8).

Your spiritual growth comes as a result of abiding or walking with Jesus. When you read, study, meditate, and memorize God's Word then you know what is expected of you. Moreover, it becomes vital to employ what you've learned. Commit to learning and applying God's Word, and you will energize those entrusted with your soul care.

The second following employment point is directed to those who are making disciples for Jesus: *Thank God for the saints' growth while seeking their complete maturity* (vv. 9–10). Paul takes up important writing space to share his thankfulness for the growth of the saints. Similarly, we should never be too busy to thank God for others. Your assignment is to read and meditate upon Philippians 1:3–6 and ask the Lord to cultivate the same attitude that Paul displays.

Furthermore, you must strive to bring those entrusted to your spiritual care to maturity. Turn to Ephesians 4:11–16 and contemplate the role of spiritual leaders and how they are called to perfect the saints. If your heart isn't aligned with the Father's heart in this matter, then have Him adjust it for you. Employing these two points will help stabilize the local church for the glory of God!

CHAPTER EIGHT

PRAYERS FOR A
RETURN TRIP AND THE
SAINTS NOT TO TRIP

1 Thessalonians 3:11–13

A husband and his wife were returning to their seats in a theater. The man said to the person seated, "I beg your pardon, but did I step on your toes when I left?"

The annoyed person sitting said, "You certainly did!"

The man standing then turned to his wife and said, "Honey, come on through, we're in the right row!"

Paul desires to return to Thessalonica; however, the wicked one puts a roadblock in the way (1 Thess. 2:18). Today's text (3:11–13) builds upon Paul's heart desire to again minister to these precious saints (3:9–10). Here are two questions to ponder before reading the holy Word of God: How should you pray for your disciples when you are physically thwarted from visiting them? Also, what should you pray for the saints spiritually when you physically cannot visit?

Now may our God and Father Himself, and our Lord Jesus Christ, direct our way to you.

And may the Lord make you increase and abound in love to one another and to all, just as we do to you, so that He may establish your hearts blameless in holiness before our God and Father at the coming of our Lord Jesus Christ with all His saints. (1 Thess. 3:11–13)

Now may our God and Father Himself and Jesus our Lord direct our way to you; and may the Lord cause you to increase and abound in love for one another, and for all people, just as we also do for you; so that He may establish your hearts without blame in holiness before our God and Father at the coming of our Lord Jesus with all His saints. (1 Thess. 3:11–13, NASB)

PREPARING THE SAINTS FOR GUESTS – F

- What function does the conjunction "now" serve (v. 11)?
- What is the antecedent of "Himself" (v. 11)?
- Does Paul as an apostle forcefully tell the Lord to "direct our way" (v. 11)?
- Are believers ever to be satisfied with their output of love (1:3; 3:12)?
- How important is the standard of "holiness" to Paul (v. 13)?
- When will we be completely holy (v. 13)?

PREPARING THE SAINTS FOR GUESTS – I

Paul has some wishes, or you might say prayers, for the missionary team and then the Thessalonian saints. "Now may our God and Father Himself, and our Lord Jesus Christ, direct our way to you" (v. 11). The conjunction "now" is transitional. The apostle then elaborates upon 1 Thessalonians 3:9–10. One article ("the") connects both the Father and Son as objects of his prayer. Observe that the text doesn't say to "the God and Father," but "our God and Father," showing the personal relationship Paul, Silas, and Timothy enjoy with the first two members of the Trinity.

"Himself" stands emphatically placed as the first word in the Greek sentence (verse). Most commentators believe it applies emphatically to the Father, but it is possible that the pronoun points to the Father and Son. As we will see, the Father and Son make a compound subject but the verb is singular, which demonstrates their unity. Jesus similarly recognizes their unity when He says, "I and My Father are one" (John 10:30). Clearly the apostle prays to the Son just as to the Father; the designation "and our Lord Jesus Christ" expresses the equality of Jesus with God the Father. Jesus is called "Lord," which is a common expression for God from the Old Testament, also expressing His full deity.

"Direct" occurs as an optative, which is a less forceful mood (or mode) than the commonly used subjunctive, and states a wish. Moreover, the verbal form is singular, displaying the oneness of the Father and Son. Since Paul writes about prayer and the maturity of the saints, it is stunning that the deity of the Father and Son is given even when the topic of the passage doesn't specifically pertain to the deity of Jesus!

"And may the Lord make you increase and abound in love to one another and to all, just as we do to you" (v. 12). Perhaps "and" would be better translated "but," since the adversative conjunction better fits the context. "But" expresses that regardless of what occurs concerning Paul's hopeful visit to Thessalonica, he desires them to grow spiritually. Also, the "you" is emphatic (it is placed first in the Greek sentence), bolstering the contrast of Paul's desired visit with the spiritual growth of the Thessalonians.

"The Lord" possibly refers to the Father as in 1 Thessalonians 3:8. Commonly from the Old Testament usage, "the Lord" standing alone refers to the Father. Yet "Lord" here seems to point to Jesus and the prayer directed to Him, as does the previous verse—Lord Jesus Christ. Another optative (wish) is offered by Paul by the words "make you increase." *To possess* or *cause to have more* communicates the meaning of the Greek optative. The apostle also desires them to "abound," which consists of having *an overabundance* or *superabundance*. Paul uses the term causatively, which conveys *to cause you to have a superabundance*. Elsewhere Paul applies the term to grace (2 Cor. 9:8) and wisdom and prudence (Eph. 1:8). In our current text Paul wishes that these saints have an overabundance of love. "Make you increase and abound" are basically synonymous. Combined, the concept is to cause to increase and overflow.

The focus of the increase and overflow is now given: love. Paul had previously praised the saints for their "labor of love" (1 Thess. 1:3). Now he desires for it to flourish in their lives, unlike those character-ized by Jesus in the latter times, "And because lawlessness will abound, the love of many will grow cold" (Matt. 24:12). These believers are to increase their love "to one another." Our Lord calls for this very practice. "By this all will know that you are My disciples," states Jesus shortly before dying, "if you have love for one another" (John 13:35). Likewise Peter shares, "And above all things have fervent love for one another, for love will cover a multitude of sins" (1 Pet. 4:8). Loving one another would be essential for Jesus' immediate disciples (and future generations) because the world would hate them and manifest their vitriol through persecution.

Paul establishes the priority of "love to one another," but broad-ens the outreach: "and to all." Love should first be directed to the saints, but then also to the unsaved. To the Galatian saints Paul declares, "Therefore, as we have opportunity, let us do good to all, especially to those who are of the household of faith" (Gal. 6:10). Paul, Silas, and Timothy had previously modeled this pattern, which is communicated by the words "just as we do to you." As Paul writes to these saints from Corinth, twice he expresses to the believers in his immediate vicinity the need of imitation. "Therefore I urge you, imitate me" (1 Cor. 4:16), and "Imitate me, just as I also imitate Christ" (1 Cor. 11:1).

The apostle gives a purpose statement, writing, "so that He may establish your hearts blameless in holiness before our God and Father at the coming of our Lord Jesus Christ with all His saints" (v. 13). His purpose for the saints to increase and abound in love is now given. "Establish" means to make firm or fixed. It first surfaces from the Greek New Testament about Jesus "that He steadfastly set [established, or firmly fixed] His face to go to Jerusalem" (Luke 9:51). In 1 Thessalonians 3:2 we learned that Timothy was dispatched to Thessalonica to "establish you and encourage you concerning your faith." Ultimately Paul trusts Jesus to keep them firm in the faith (2 Thess. 2:17; 3:3).

Paul's goal is to firmly fix or establish their lives to be "blameless." *Without fault* is the literal meaning of this term found five times from the Greek New Testament. Luke records about Zacharias and Elizabeth, "And they were both righteous before God, walking in all the commandments and ordinances of the Lord blameless" (Luke 1:6). God honors the godly parents with a son who would walk in their footsteps: John the Baptist. Specifically, Paul longs for the saints to be "blameless in holiness." The feminine noun "holiness" points to the state and not the process of sanctification; it only occurs elsewhere in Romans 1:4 and 2 Corinthians 7:1.

There is no contradiction when Paul writes, "before our God and Father at the coming of Jesus" and his earlier statement "in the presence of our Lord Jesus Christ at His coming" (2:19). We've seen the linkage between the compound subject Father and Son even by the singular verb "direct," which closely affixes the eternal duo (3:11). Moreover, the definite article ("the") connects "our God and Father," articulating one person with two titles. The timing for the desired holiness is "at the coming of the Lord Jesus Christ." *To come to a place* or *make a visit* conveys the origin of "coming." Paul uses this term of the Rapture in 1 Thessalonians 4:15 as does John in 1 John 2:28. "And thus we shall always be with the Lord" adds Paul in 1 Thessalonians 4:17. Jesus' personal visit or appearance will be "with all His saints." The term "holy" can refer to "holy angels" (Matt. 25:31) but the context better appeals to church-age saints, as in 1 Thessalonians 4:14–17. Church-age believers who are described as "the dead in Christ" will return with Jesus (1 Thess. 4:16).

Amazing how much theology is communicated in just three Bible verses. The Scripture intricately links many topics like we just examined. Let's further probe the eternal Word through relationship.

PREPARING THE SAINTS FOR GUESTS – R

Sadly, there has been a mockery of both the Father and Son in modern Christianity. Instead of viewing the two members of the Trinity as sovereignly building the church, many believe the Father and Son are to be commanded to bring them personal success—as if the Father and Son are marionettes, and we pull the strings. Bad theology has taken root in certain Christian circles, leading to blasphemous practices.

For instance, Matthew 18:19 has been severed from its context of discipline and has been deemed a text about prayer. Jesus says, "Again I say to you that if two of you agree on earth concerning anything that they ask, it will be done for them by My Father in heaven." According to current practice all that two or three believers need to do is agree what God must do for them, and in prayer bind God to grant them their wish. Clearly the steps for discipline are given by Jesus, and not principles to bind God in prayer (Matt. 18:15–20). We are never given any Scriptural mandate for such unscrupulous practices.

Consider Paul, who's an apostle. If anyone would seem to have the ability to command the Lord, it would be one with apostolic authority. Yet Paul does not tell the Lord to do anything, but rather submits to His sovereignty. Read carefully about his thorn in the flesh and how the suffering apostle approaches the throne of grace (2 Cor. 12:1–10).

Moreover, consider Peter, who was one of the inner circle along with James and John. He gives a wonderful confession of Jesus' deity, "You are the Christ, the Son of the living God" (Matt. 16:16), and subsequently tells Jesus that He cannot go to the cross. Read carefully how he confronts the Lord, "Then Peter took Him aside and began to rebuke Him, saying, 'Far be it from You, Lord; this shall not happen to You!'" (Matt. 16:22). How does Jesus respond? "But He turned and said to Peter, 'Get behind Me, Satan! You are an offense to Me, for you are not mindful of the things of God, but the things of men'" (Matt. 16:23).

Finally, how did the eternal Son of God address His Father in the garden of Gethsemane? Jesus humbly prays, "Father, if it is Your will, take this cup away from Me; nevertheless not My will, but Yours, be done" (Luke 22:42). The precious Son of Man entreats His loving Father with the utmost respect, and so should we!

Be cautious, my beloved brother and sister in Christ; many today are embracing doctrines that do not align with the holy Scriptures and will put you on a collision course with the Lord. Remember to always pray: not my will be done, but Yours!

PREPARING THE SAINTS FOR GUESTS – E

We are called to serve one another in the body of Christ (1 Pet. 4:10–11). For this reason Christians have to be with other Christians to help them grow. *Ask the Lord to clear a path to the saints* (v. 11) is our first employment point. Satan seeks to keep us from those whom we are to serve (1 Thess. 2:18). Prayer becomes a power tool in the saint's hands to open up doors for ministry. Humbly Paul pursues an open door through prayer to care for the spiritual needs of the Thessalonians. Let's get down on our knees and pray for those we are called to help in ministry, so that we may have access to them in order to build them up in Christ.

Jesus is coming again; we only have a limited time to shepherd the treasured saints whom He has entrusted to us. *Ask the Lord to mature the saints for Jesus' arrival* (vv. 12–13) gives us employment point number two. Paul transitions from praying for his missionary team (v. 11) to now intercede for the saints at Thessalonica (vv. 12–13). His goal consists of their maturity. So set aside time daily to pray for those you mentor to increase in love and holiness. These primary two character qualities are essential for the development of believers. Purpose to have them mature in these two areas, so that they will be ready to stand before Judge Jesus at the Rapture!

PART TWO

REQUIREMENTS FOR THE FUTURE

1 Thessalonians 4:1–5:28

CHAPTER NINE

THE NECESSITY TO WALK IN GOD'S WAY AND WILL

1 Thessalonians 4:1–8

There was a man who, at age seventy, loved to golf. He was of a sound body. He could really drive a golf ball. Yet he had poor vision and couldn't see where the ball went. One day he came up with a solution. The elderly gentleman went to the clubhouse and said to the people there that he would generously pay someone with above average eyesight who could see where his ball went.

An elderly man, who was eighty years old, told the avid golfer that he had 20/20 vision and would be glad to do the job. They both went to the course, and the golfer drove the golf ball a long way. He asked his elderly counterpart if he saw where the ball went. The eighty-year-old man said, "I did." The golfer asked him to show him where the ball was. The elderly man said he couldn't. Then the golfer asked, "Didn't you see it?" He replied, "Yes, but I forgot where it was."

Thankfully the Thessalonian saints heard and heeded (by remembering) the teachings of Paul during his brief stay with them. Yet they were charged to increase spiritually in their walk and service to Jesus.

Let me share with you two focus questions before reading the sacred text: What should thriving spiritual Christians do to keep maturing? And, how are you to honor God's will for your life?

Finally then, brethren, we urge and exhort in the Lord Jesus that you abound more and more, just as you received from us how you ought to walk and to please God; for you know what commandments we gave you through the Lord Jesus.

For this is the will of God, your sanctification: that you should abstain from sexual immorality; that each of you should know how to possess his own vessel in sanctification and honor, not in passion of lust, like the Gentiles who do not know God; that no one should take advantage of and defraud his brother in this matter, because the Lord is the avenger of all such, as we also forewarned you and testified. For God did not call us to uncleanness, but in holiness. Therefore he who rejects this does not reject man, but God, who has also given us His Holy Spirit. (1 Thess. 4:1–8)

As for other matters, brothers and sisters, we instructed you how to live in order to please God, as in fact you are living. Now we ask you and urge you in the Lord Jesus to do this more and more. For you know what instructions we gave you by the authority of the Lord Jesus.

It is God's will that you should be sanctified: that you should avoid sexual immorality; that each of you should learn to control your own body in a way that is holy and honorable, not in passionate lust like the pagans, who do not know God; and that in this matter no one should wrong or take advantage of a brother or sister. The Lord will punish all those who commit such sins, as we told you and warned you before. For God did not call us to be impure, but to live a holy life. Therefore, anyone who rejects this instruction does not reject a human being but God, the very God who gives you his Holy Spirit. (1 Thess. 4:1–8, NIV)

GOD'S WILL FOR YOU – F

"Finally then, brethren, we urge and exhort in the Lord Jesus that you should abound more and more, just as you received from us how you ought to walk and to please God" (v. 1). The adjective "finally" appears fourteen times from the Greek New Testament, meaning *as for the rest*. It is not a conclusion but a movement toward the end of the letter, and can indicate a brief ending (2 Cor. 13:11) or extended closing (Phil. 3:1). "Then" draws upon the previous text (3:13) with an upcoming exhortation. Again Paul uses the affectionate "brethren" to introduce his plea.

In classical Greek the verb "urge" only referred to a question, and subsequently of making a request. Paul employs the term making an appeal as a caring friend. The apostle uses two terms ("urge and exhort"), adding strength to the appeal. Both verbs occur in the present tense, showing linear action. "Exhort" carries the notion of *being called alongside*. Interestingly, Paul places "you" (in the Greek) between the two verbs; there are three general interpretations to the location of "you."

First, "you" links both verbs with "in the Lord Jesus," so the dual exhortations are made with Jesus' authority. Yet Paul makes a personal appeal, using "urge" in 1 Thessalonians 5:12 and 2 Thessalonians 2:1; without "exhort" showing, the two terms are not equated and "urge" emerges in all three passages (1 Thess. 4:1; 5:12; 2 Thess. 2:1) as appeals from a friend. Others see "urge" as an appeal from friends and the latter "exhort" connecting "in the Lord Jesus." They reason that each has its own modifier. So, "we urge you [as friends] and exhort in the Lord Jesus." However, "exhort" occurs in other letters by Paul, making a personal exhortation in teaching portions of his epistles (Rom. 12:1; Eph. 4:1). These are stronger than to "urge" (an appeal) but not to the level of a command.

Three, "in the Lord Jesus" seems best to go with the following exhortation and not with "urge" and "exhort." The concept is that "we urge you [as friend to friend] and exhort." There is a break in thought and "in the [realm or sphere of the] Lord Jesus that you should abound more and more" is a separate unit of thought. The general exhortation to these saints is that they *be excessive,* which is the meaning of "abound." Paul then keeps piling on with "more and more."

The Thessalonians saints had "received from us [Paul, Silas, and Timothy] how you ought to walk and to please God." *To take* or *to receive* conveys the meaning of the verb "received." In 1 Thessalonians 2:13 the taking or receiving is used of biblical instruction (from teacher to apprentice) and of ethical guidance in 2 Thessalonians 3:6. The definite article ("the") ties "how you ought to walk and to please God" as the object of the verb "received."

Also, the same article ("the") governs the two infinitives "to walk" and "to please." Previously Paul had addressed the term "walk," which speaks about one's lifestyle: "that you would walk worthy of God who calls you into His own kingdom and glory" (1 Thess. 2:12). Later he exhorts the saints about appropriate Christian living before the unjust, "that you may walk properly toward those who are outside" (1 Thess. 4:12). Jesus, being "the Way" has modeled for us how to walk. John records Jesus saying, "I am the way, the truth, and the life" (John 14:6). The early church was called "the Way" (Acts 9:2; 19:23; 24:22). Paul wants the believers to imitate Jesus and walk in the Way!

The root meaning of "to please" is *to fit* or *adapt*. So *to fit* or *adapt* to walk with the Lord is to please Him. People *fit* or *adapt* themselves to please others or God. Matthew gives us the first of seventeen uses of "to please," showing a negative example: "But when Herod's birthday was celebrated, the daughter of Herodias danced before them and pleased [adapted or fitted herself] Herod" (Matt. 14:6). Conversely, Paul gives us the last New Testament occurrence of "to please" in 2 Timothy 2:4: "No one engaged in warfare entangles himself with the affairs of this life, that he may please him who enlisted him as a soldier." Let's *adapt* or *fit* our lives to please God by keeping Jesus' way and Word!

"For you know what commandments we gave you through the Lord Jesus," writes Paul (v. 2). The conjunction "for" connects the remainder of our passage (vv. 2–8) with that which was previously stated (v. 1) whereas "you know" draws the saints back to Paul's earlier instruction while he was with them. *To announce alongside of* relays the meaning of "commandments," which arises five times from the Greek New Testament. It transmits the imagery of giving an announcement to someone in close proximity (Acts 5:28; 16:24; 1 Tim. 1:5, 18). Paul's up-close and personal commands are marked with the Lord's authority, since they are "through the Lord Jesus."

Paul gives us another "for" to begin the verse, which ties together his general exhortation for spiritual growth (vv. 1–2) with refraining from sexual immorality: "For this is the will of God, your sanctification: that you should abstain from sexual immorality" (v. 3). There exists no article before "will of God," so Paul does not cover everything that is in God's will but one specific aspect. "Will" speaks of *an inclination of that which is liked.* It expresses the will, wish, volition, or purpose. The Greek ending *ma* upon the term shows the *result* of the will. The first of sixty-four appearances consists of Jesus' words instructing His disciples how to pray with the renowned statement, "Your will be done" (Matt. 6:10).

An essential component of God's will is "your sanctification." Paul places the term appositionally (side by side) with the "will of God." There are three aspects of sanctification: positional, progressive, and pending. Since saints are positionally seated with Christ (Eph. 1:3; 2:6), we are blessed with enormous and incalculable spiritual blessings. Daily we are to move forward in holiness, which is described by progressive sanctification (Heb. 12:14). Then when the process is complete (characterized by the term "pending") we will be fully conformed to the image of God.

Children of God are to "abstain" from sexual sin. The epexegetical infinitive explains more fully the nature of sanctification. Luke first uses the term in Acts 15:20 (and shortly thereafter a second time in Acts 15:29) in the context of the Jerusalem council, where exhortations are offered to the saints to refrain from idol worship and sexual immorality.

"Sexual immorality" refers to *fornication* or *to commit sexual sin.* Paul labels it as a work of the flesh in Galatians 5:19. We will probe this topic in greater detail under relationship.

"That each of you should know how to possess his own vessel in sanctification and honor," continues Paul (v. 4). The words translated "should know" come from one Greek word. Most likely it is an epexegetical infinitive more fully elaborating upon the practice of purity. The classical Greek meaning of "to possess" denotes *to procure* or *acquire*. Indeed the present tense in the papyri (secular documents in that period of time) does the same. Therefore the present infinitive translated "to possess" in 1 Thessalonians 4:4 accurately relays *to possess* "his own vessel." The meaning of "vessel" has been debated throughout church history.

First Peter 3:7 is the text regularly referred to as showing evidence the "vessel" points to a wife. Peter writes, "giving honor to the wife, as to the weaker vessel," but the verse doesn't say he possesses her. The term "vessel" emerges figuratively of the human body as "earthen vessels" (2 Cor. 4:7). Also, you have David speaking about the men's bodies that are with him, declaring that "the vessels of the young men are holy" in 1 Samuel 21:5. (The term "vessel" appears in 1 Samuel 21:6 of the Greek Septuagint, which is traditionally referred to as LXX.) Remember that our context is Paul's exhortation for moral purity, so "to possess his own vessel" best describes the saints of Thessalonica, who are to control their own bodies for God's glory.

Paul calls the believers to manage their own bodies "in sanctification and honor." Once again the apostle uses the term "sanctification" (1 Thess. 4:3), and conveys that it "is the will of God." He employs the term "honor," and the feminine noun transmits the meaning *to give* or *pay homage, value and respect*. Judas betrays Jesus; "the price [honor or value] of blood" (Matt. 27:6) is cited as "thirty pieces of silver" (Matt. 27:9). The saint is to manage his own body to be holy and valuable!

"Not in passion of lust," writes Paul concerning the discipline of the body, "like the Gentiles who do not know God" (v. 5). Paul is the only one who uses the noun "passion," and gives us all three uses from the Greek New Testament. Concerning fallen mankind, the apostle refers to "vile passions" in Romans 1:26, and places the term between "uncleanness" and "evil desire" in Colossians 3:5 about the members of the body that need to be put to death. The "passion of lust" described in 1 Thessalonians 4:5 continues the biblical narrative of all three negative uses of "passion." Thirty-eight times the Greek word for "lust" materializes in the New Testament; it can be applied to a good desire (Luke 22:15) or bad one (1 John 2:15–17). Paul's employment of the term in 1 Thessalonians 4:5 has the latter use.

Believers are not to be just "like the Gentiles who do not know God." The Gentiles in our passage point to non-Jewish people who are idolaters, not knowing the true God. Paul, who writes from the immoral city of Corinth, attributes such wicked practices as incest (1 Cor. 5:1) and idolatry (1 Cor. 10:20) to the Gentiles.

Unlike the Gentiles who know no limits to their immoral practices, the saints are to lead holy lives. "That no one should take advantage of and defraud his brother in this matter, because the Lord is the avenger of all such, as we also forewarned you and testified (v. 6). *To go beyond* imparts the literal meaning of the present infinitive "should take advantage," which only surfaces here from the Greek New Testament. Paul warns the saints not to cross a moral boundary and sin against God and "defraud his brother." The term "defraud" derives from two words meaning *I have more*. Both Paul (2 Cor. 12:17) and Titus (2 Cor. 12:18) never defrauded the saints at Corinth, and now the Thessalonians should not take advantage of others.

"In this matter" carries the notion of *something to be done* and is used euphemistically of sexual immorality. Paul cites a reason to dissuade the saints from violating their brethren, "because the Lord is the avenger of all such." Most likely "the Lord" here refers to Jesus, as He is referred to as "the Lord Jesus" in 1 Thessalonians 4:2. He is described as "the avenger," which only appears here and in Hebrews 13:4. The anonymous writer of Hebrews pens, "Marriage is honorable among all, and the bed undefiled; but fornicators and adulterers God will judge." Previously Paul had taught the saints this lesson as shown by the words "as we also forewarned you and testified."

"Not" stands first in the Greek sentence for emphasis when Paul writes, "For God did not call us to uncleanness, but in holiness." The "for" connects with Jesus as the Judge (v. 6) and shows the reason (v. 7) not to imitate Gentile practices. Also, for the third time the root of "holiness" and "sanctification" is given (vv. 3, 4, 7).

"Therefore he who rejects this does not reject man, but God, who has also given us His Holy Spirit" (v. 8). The inferential conjunction "therefore" draws a conclusion based upon the previous information. Paul warns the saints that the individual "who rejects" his teaching spurns God's authority—not only that, but the same "God who has given us His Spirit." Therefore, rejecting Paul's teaching is to reject God who gave us the Holy Spirit. To do so is to invite Jesus to avenge the ungodly activity.

Now that we have interpreted 1 Thessalonians 4:1–8, let us use the lens of Scripture to enlarge our understanding.

GOD'S WILL FOR YOU – R

Greeks did not hold the body in high esteem. Many were taught dualism, which is the belief that the spirit is good but anything material is bad; since the body is material, it should not be revered. Paul writes from Corinth; the city's name carried the reputation of fornication and immorality. Dualism had permeated the thinking of the region, so the apostle has to reeducate the saints about the sanctity of the body. He writes, "Or do you not know that your body is the temple of the Holy Spirit who is in you, whom you have from God, and you are not your own? For you were bought at a price; therefore glorify God in your body and in your spirit, which are God's" (1 Cor. 6:19–20). Jesus paid a hefty price to redeem us (His life and the sacrifice of His blood). We have been purchased out of the slave market of sin, and now belong to Him: spirit, soul, and body!

The gross immorality in the pagan world should not be envied nor practiced by believers. Consider Paul's verbal scourging of the saints at Corinth, "It is actually reported that there is sexual immorality among you, and such sexual immorality as is not even named among the Gentiles—that a man has his father's wife!" (1 Cor. 5:1). As Paul writes the above situation existed; the present tense verb "has" shows the continuation of this debauchery.

God has redeemed the entire man; therefore, Paul commands the saints not to defile themselves through sexual immorality. Toward the end of 1 Thessalonians he states, "Now may the God of peace Himself sanctify you completely; and may your whole spirit, soul, and body be preserved blameless at the coming of our Lord Jesus Christ" (5:23). We can have confidence that what God has started in our lives He will fulfill. First Thessalonians 5:24 offers, "He who calls you is faithful, who also will do it."

GOD'S WILL FOR YOU – E

Excel spiritually to please God by walking with Him, and keeping His commandments (vv. 1–2) is our first employment point. Great men and women of God walk with Him. Prior to the flood Enoch had a special relationship with the Lord. In the midst of a wicked world, Moses writes, "And Enoch walked with God; and he was not, for God took him" (Gen. 5:24). The writer of Hebrews lists Enoch among the heroes of faith. He pens, "By faith Enoch was taken away so that he did not see death, and was not found, because God had taken him, for before he was taken he had this testimony, that he pleased God" (Heb. 11:5). To please God is to walk with Him. Then we also have Noah; "This is the genealogy of Noah. Noah was a just man, perfect in his generations. Noah walked with God" (Gen. 6:9).

Your assignment is first to write out Ephesians 4:1–3 on a small index card and then throughout the day consider the following: "I, therefore, the prisoner of the Lord, beseech you to walk worthy of the calling with which you were called, with all lowliness, and gentleness, with longsuffering, bearing with one another in love, endeavoring to keep the unity of the Spirit in the bond of peace." Then, write out 1 John 5:3 on the back of that card and do the same. The apostle of love writes, "For this is the love of God, that we keep His commandments. And His commandments are not burdensome." Ask the Lord throughout the day to help you walk with Him by practicing His commandments!

Next, let the words of the apostle Paul challenge you in the area of holiness: *Esteem God's will through holy living* (vv. 3–8), employment point number two. You are to focus upon God's will for your life. To practice the known will of God (that which is communicated in His Word) ensures that the Lord guides us in the everyday affairs of life. Memorize 1 Thessalonians 4:3, seeking to implement its necessary guidance. "For this is the will of God," writes the apostle Paul by the inspiration of the Spirit of God, "that you should abstain from sexual immorality." So, let's walk with Him, keep the commandments, and please the Lord through holy living!

CHAPTER TEN

THE TRUE EXPANSION OF PHILADELPHIA (BROTHERLY LOVE)

1 Thessalonians 4:9–12

A pastor regularly visited church members on a bicycle. One day while on his bicycle he noticed a boy trying to sell a lawn mower. The minister asked, "How much do you want for the mower?"

Quickly the little fellow replied, "I just want enough money to go out and buy me a bicycle."

The pastor pondered the situation for a moment and replied with the following: "Will you trade the lawn mower for my bicycle?" Wisely, the small boy asked if he could try it out first, and after riding the bike up and down the street said, "Sir, you've got yourself a deal."

The happy minister took the mower and primed the gasoline. Then he pulled on the rope a few times with no response from the mower. The preacher called the little boy over and said, "I can't get this mower to start."

Then the little boy said, "That's because you have to cuss at it to get it started."

Surprised the pastor replied, "I'm a minister, and I can't cuss. It has been so long since I've been saved that I don't even remember how to cuss."

The bold little one looked at him, smiling. "Just keep pulling on that string. It'll come back to you."

Amazingly after the Thessalonian saints endured severe trials, cussing didn't proceed from their mouths, but brotherly love from their lives. Here are two questions for your consideration just before looking at 1 Thessalonians 4:9–12: How should biblical brotherly love (the Greek word gives us the name "Philadelphia") function? Should we give up secular employment, since Jesus is returning?

But concerning brotherly love you have no need that I should write to you, for you yourselves are taught by God to love one another; and indeed you do so toward all the brethren who are in all Macedonia. But we urge you, brethren, that you increase more and more; that you also aspire to lead a quiet life, to mind your own business, and to work with your own hands, as we commanded you, that you may walk properly toward those who are outside, and that you may lack nothing. (1 Thess. 4:9–12)

We don't have to write you about the need to love each other. God has taught you to do this, and you already have shown your love for all of his people in Macedonia. But, my dear friends, we ask you to do even more. Try your best to live quietly, to mind your own business, and to work hard, just as we taught you to do. Then you will be respected by people who are not followers of the Lord, and you won't have to depend on anyone. (1 Thess. 4:9–12, CEV)

WIDE-RANGE LOVING WHILE LOVING QUIET LIVING – F

- What do the words "but concerning" reveal (v. 9)?
- How did God teach the saints "to love one another" (v. 9)?
- Why are the saints commanded to "increase more and more" in love (v. 10)?
- What do the words "to mind your own business" mean (v. 11)?
- Why is "to work with your own hands" anti-cultural (v. 11)?
- Who might be impacted negatively by a poor work ethic (v. 12)?

WIDE-RANGE LOVING WHILE LOVING QUIET LIVING – I

"But concerning brotherly love you have no need that I should write to you, for you yourselves are taught by God to love one another," pens Paul. The opening two words "but concerning" mark the beginning of a new section (see also 1 Thess. 5:1; 1 Cor. 7:1; 8:1; 12:1; 16:1). Outside of the Greek New Testament "brotherly love" is used of family (biological) members. All six New Testament uses of the noun enter into the picture of those related to one another through Jesus (Rom. 12:10; Heb. 13:1; 1 Pet. 1:22; 2 Pet. 1:7 [twice]).

The reason "you have no need that I should write to you" is given: "for you yourselves are taught by God to love one another." Paul stresses the Thessalonian saints' love by the emphatic "you yourselves." The curious expression "taught by God" arises only here from the Greek New Testament and further clarifies Paul's rationale, expressing their love. Although the adjective appears only here, a similar term arises in John 6:45. Jesus says, "It is written in the prophets, 'And they shall all be taught by God,'" which comes from Isaiah 54:13 and Micah 4:2. Saints have an inner witness and teacher through the Holy Spirit. Paul writes, "These things we also speak, not in words which man's wisdom teaches but which the Holy Spirit teaches, comparing spiritual things with spiritual" (1 Cor. 2:13).

God teaches saints through the indwelling Holy Spirit "to love one another," which expression is introduced through a purpose construction from the Greek. In other words, you are God's student for the purpose of loving one another. "To love" derives from an infinitive in the present tense. The saints are to continually love one another as they have received instruction from God. This meshes with Leviticus 19:18, which is often quoted from in the New Testament. Moses pens, "but you shall love your neighbor as yourself."

The apostle cites the following reference for the saints' love: "and indeed you do so toward all the brethren who are in all Macedonia. But we urge you, brethren, that you increase more and more" (v. 10). Paul's use of "and" looks back to the previous statement about believers being "taught by God"; and "indeed," which would better be translated "for," looks forward to the evidence now presented. "You so do" points to "love one another," and "toward all the brethren who are in Macedonia" would include the saints in Philippi and Berea and perhaps to other churches we don't know about. One thing we know for sure is that the saints in the region had personally experienced the love of the Thessalonians.

An exhortation to keep on practicing love for one another is expressed through the present tense verb "urge." Paul's warm pastoral heart again emerges through the term "brethren." He desires them *to excel beyond a set number* or *boundary*, which is the meaning of the term "increase." The comparative adverb "more" only enhances the apostle's desire for the increase of love to one another.

We receive a hint concerning one of Paul's troubles with certain of the saints. He writes, "that you also aspire to lead a quiet life, to mind your own business, and to work with your own hands, as we commanded you" (v. 12). The present infinitive "aspire" literally states *to love honor* and refers to one's aim or ambition. The goal-oriented apostle uses the term first in Romans 15:20: "And so I have made it my aim [translated "aspire" in 1 Thessalonians 4:11] to preach the gospel, not where Christ was named, lest I should build on another man's foundation." Next it occurs in 2 Corinthians 5:9 where Paul writes, "Therefore we make it our aim, whether present [with the Lord; 2 Cor. 5:8] or absent [from the Lord; 2 Cor. 5:6], to be well pleasing to Him."

Paul's aim or ambition for these saints is "that you aspire to lead a quiet life." *To be quiet* or *rest from work* gives the meaning of the term "quiet." Doctor Luke first uses the term of a healed man with dropsy whom the Lord restores on the Sabbath. He records about the spectators' response to Jesus confronting the hypocrites: "But they kept silent" (Luke 14:4). Then again Luke uses the term concerning the women who went to Jesus' tomb just prior to the Sabbath: "And they rested on the Sabbath according to the commandment" (Luke 23:56).

Moreover, Paul desires the saints "to mind your own business." His rhetoric intensifies in 2 Thessalonians 3:11–12. "For we hear that there are some who walk among you in a disorderly manner," chides the disturbed apostle about the report, "not working at all, but are busybodies. Now those who are such we command and exhort through our Lord Jesus Christ that they work in quietness and eat their own bread." He desires them "to work with your own hands." Paul strongly points out in 2 Thessalonians 3:10," For even when we were with you, we commanded you this: If anyone will not work, neither shall he eat." In Ephesians Paul prescribes the following: "Let him who stole steal no longer, but rather let him labor, working with his own hands what is good, that he may have something to give him who has need" (Eph. 4:28). Paul closes the verse declaring not his opinion but authority, "as we commanded you."

Wisely the apostle lays out two reasons why the saints should provide for themselves: "that you may walk properly toward those who are outside, and that you may lack nothing" (v. 12). As the saints were previously counseled to "walk worthy of God" (1 Thess. 2:12), now likewise they are to have a good testimony to the unsaved. That is purpose number one. The second purpose is "that you may lack nothing." The word "nothing" can be masculine, meaning "no one," which would show that they are not dependent upon the provision of others; or the neuter, which conveys "nothing." Option number two is better, because it goes with "have need" and usually refers to something that is needed.

Great! We have just walked through the passage, interpreting its meaning. Now we are going to probe its extended implications.

WIDE-RANGE LOVING WHILE LOVING QUIET LIVING – R

God is our best teacher. Paul demonstrates this truth by 1 Thessalonians 4:9, "But concerning brotherly love you have no need that I should write to you, for you yourselves are taught by God to love one another." The Lord diversifies the ways His children are taught;

however, make no mistake that ultimately He is the One who imparts many wonderful truths to us through His Word!

Jesus is truly the Master-Teacher. The Sermon on the Mount grants us the best sermon ever preached. Like the giving of the Law, our Lord's sermon was delivered from a mountain. When the Word of God is elevated, then the people of God are humbled. Observe that Jesus' sermon begins as follows: "Blessed are the poor in spirit, for theirs is the kingdom of God" (Matt. 5:3). The Bible message, when given its proper place, rightly humbles people by its inherent power. "Poor" conveys the idea of a *beggar with great needs*, which leads to mourning over one's personal sin. "Blessed are those who mourn," continues Jesus, "For they shall be comforted" (Matt. 5:4).

Yet the greatest instructor who ever walked on planet Earth only ministered for a little more than three years. How would God's children then be taught? As Jesus plans to return to the Father, He says, "And I will pray the Father, and He will give you another Helper, that He may abide with you forever—the Spirit of truth, whom the world cannot receive, because it neither sees Him nor knows Him; but you know Him, for He dwells with you and will be in you" (John 14:16–17). The Greek word for "another" in "another Helper" means *another of the same kind*. Jesus will dispatch the third member of the Godhead after arriving in heaven, and the Holy Spirit will then indwell believers and be God's personal teacher to them.

In conjunction with Jesus' ascension would be the impartation of gifts to the body of Christ (the church). These gifts are actually gifted men whom the Lord will use to mature the saints through the teaching of the Scripture. Paul writes, "And He Himself [Jesus] gave some to be apostles, some prophets, some evangelists, and some pastors and teachers, for the equipping of the saints for the work of ministry, for the edifying of the body of Christ, till we all come to the unity of the faith and of the knowledge of the Son of God, to a perfect man, to the measure of the stature of the fullness of Christ" (Eph. 4:11–13).

Therefore the Thessalonian saints clearly "are taught by God to love one another" (1 Thess. 4:9). God in His sovereignty trains us as

Jesus did His apprentices; the Spirit of truth indwelling us guides us into truth, also using gifted men (who are gifts to us) so that we may be firmly grounded in the faith.

Are you ready to go to work? Truly it is a blessing to become familiar with the text, interpret it accurately, see its wider implications, and then employ it personally.

WIDE-RANGE LOVING WHILE LOVING QUIET LIVING – E

How pleasing must the Thessalonian saints been to Paul. Receiving the report from Timothy about their continued growth must have been a sweet tune to the apostle's ears and heart. John's words speak volumes to all spiritual fathers in the faith. He writes, "I have no greater joy than to hear that my children walk in truth" (3 John 4). Yet the sons and daughters of God must always press forward in their love for one another and others. *Increase loving one another as God teaches you* (vv. 9–10), therefore, is our first employment point.

Faith, hope, and love are the strong character qualities of these saints. Nonetheless they need to build more spiritual muscle. As they have been "taught by God to love one another," now they must "increase more and more." Thankfully these saints heed the admonition. Second Thessalonians 1:3 testifies of their increase, "We are bound to thank God always for you, brethren, as it is fitting, because your faith grows exceedingly, and the love of every one of you all abounds toward each other." Let us go and do likewise!

Live quietly, privately, and work diligently to lack nothing maintaining a good witness (vv. 11–12) is employment point two. Take time and reflect upon your work ethic. Remember that God punched a time clock, working six days and then resting on the seventh. Just as the Lord was diligent in His work, so should we be. Moreover, the Father placed Adam in the garden of Eden not as a punishment but as a blessing. How hard do you work for the Lord? Do you spend unnecessary time talking to others when you should be working? What would your coworkers say about your job performance? It is vital that children of God work for the glory of God and don't reflect a lazy work ethic.

To the bondslaves in Ephesians 6, Paul writes, "be obedient to those who are your masters according to the flesh, with fear and trembling, in sincerity of heart, as to Christ; not with eyeservice, as menpleasers, but as bondservants of Christ, doing the will of God from the heart, with goodwill doing service, as to the Lord, and not to men" (Eph. 6:5–7). Similarly, we should work as to the Lord, not getting caught up with office politics or the gossip around the water cooler. Let's represent the Lord well!

CHAPTER ELEVEN

ENCOURAGING DETAILS
ABOUT THE RAPTURE

1 Thessalonians 4:13–18

A blink of an eye takes three hundred to four hundred milliseconds. There are a thousand milliseconds in each second, so a blink takes approximately one third of a second. Scientists have demonstrated that the average person blinks fifteen to twenty times per minute.

Imagine Paul's analogy for how quickly we will be changed at the Rapture. He pens, "Behold, I tell you a mystery: We shall not all sleep, but we shall all be changed in a moment ["moment" literally means *unable to cut*, so the time cannot be divided], in the twinkling of an eye" (1 Cor. 15:51–52). Paul had instructed the saints at Thessalonica about the Rapture, which occurs before the Tribulation. Although the apostle didn't avoid teaching new believers about eschatology (the study of the end times), 1 Thessalonians 4:13–18 (and also 1 Corinthians 15:51–58) is given to comfort the believers. An apparent concern underlies 1 Thessalonians 4:13–18.

Before we interpret the text, let's carefully read this sacred portion of Scripture.

But I do not want you to be ignorant, brethren, concerning those who have fallen asleep, lest you sorrow as others who have no hope. For if we believe that Jesus died and rose again, even so God will bring with Him those who sleep in Jesus.

For this we say to you by the word of the Lord, that we who are alive and remain until the coming of the Lord will by no means precede those who are asleep. For the Lord Himself will descend from heaven with a shout, with the voice of an archangel, and with the trumpet of God. And the dead in Christ will rise first. Then we who are alive and remain shall be caught up together with them in the clouds to meet the Lord in the air. And thus we shall always be with the Lord. Therefore comfort one another with these words. (1 Thess. 4:13–18)

But we do not want you to be uninformed, brethren, about those who are asleep, so that you will not grieve as do the rest who have no hope. For if we believe that Jesus died and rose again, even so God will bring with Him those who have fallen asleep in Jesus. For this we say to you by the word of the Lord, that we who are alive and remain until the coming of the Lord, will not precede those who have fallen asleep. For the Lord Himself will descend from heaven with a shout, with the voice of the archangel and with the trumpet of God, and the dead in Christ will rise first. Then we who are alive and remain will be caught up together with them in the clouds to meet the Lord in the air, and so we shall always be with the Lord. Therefore comfort one another with these words. (1 Thess. 4:13–18, NASB)

THE FAMILY REUNION AT THE RAPTURE – F

- What is the meaning of "I do not want you to be ignorant" (v. 13)?
- Who are the ones "who have fallen asleep" (v. 13)?
- Where does God take those "who God will bring with Him" (v. 14)?
- Are the church-age saints who die before the Rapture disadvantaged (v. 15)?
- How important is it that "the dead in Christ will rise first" (v. 16)?
- Why does Paul use the first plural "we" (vv. 15, 17)?
- What is the "therefore" there for (v. 18)?

THE FAMILY REUNION AT THE RAPTURE – I

Paul begins our passage with a common expression, "But I do not want you to be ignorant," and continues, "brethren, concerning those who have fallen asleep, lest you sorrow as others who have no hope" (v. 13). The opening formula ("I do not want you to be ignorant") introduces an important matter (Rom. 1:13; 11:25; 1 Cor. 10:1; 12:1; 2 Cor. 1:8). "But," which begins the verse, shows a transition to a new topic. Repeatedly Paul uses the term "brethren" in the Greek New Testament after the above formula in every passage cited but 1 Corinthians 12:1, which occurs before the expression.

"Concerning those who have fallen asleep" gives us the area of apprehension for the Thessalonian saints. Paul euphemistically uses "fallen asleep" for death. The term can refer to literal sleep (Matt. 28:13; John 11:11). None of the eighteen occurrences point to "soul sleep"; the erroneous doctrine labeled soul sleep teaches that the souls of those who have died remain in the condition of unconscious existence until the final resurrection.

Paul then gives us the following purpose statement after addressing the topic of concern for the saints: "lest you sorrow as others who have no hope." Theocritus writes in the third century, "Hopes are among the living; the dead are without hope." The insightful apostle doesn't want the saints to "sorrow," which appears in the present tense, showing an ongoing grief. We are not to be "as others," which refers to unbelievers "who have no hope." It is not as though the unsaved have no hope of an afterlife. Some did! Rather, Paul's point consists of the lost not knowing the true God. Paul expresses their lost condition by reminding the Ephesian saints when they were spiritually dead, "that at that time you were without Christ . . . having no hope and without God in the world" (Eph. 2:12).

"For if we believe that Jesus died and rose again, even so God will bring with Him those who sleep in Jesus" (v. 14). Paul's use of the first-class condition ("if") assumes the statement to be true. That is, the apostle affirms the saints' confidence that Jesus died and rose again. Our Lord's humanity and earthly journey are emphasized by the name "Jesus." Both verbs "died" and "rose again" are in the active voice, demonstrating that Jesus is the One who laid His life down and took it up again (John 10:17–18). The Greek verb for "died" has an intensifier (preposition) affixed to it as in 1 Thessalonians 5:10, whereas "rose again" derives from the adverb *again* and the verb *to stand*. Paul deploys the term again in 1 Thessalonians 4:16.

"Even so" connects the resurrection of Jesus with the saints' resurrection. The verb "will bring" either shows that God will bring the spirits of deceased Christians who come from heaven with Jesus to meet their resurrected bodies or God will bring at the imminent return of Christ all church-age saints, whether alive or dead, back to heaven with Jesus. Although both options are true, the latter fits the context of the passage (see 1 Thess. 3:13; 4:17; John 14:2–3).

A note of God's tender care for the sheep is expressed by the words "those who sleep in Jesus." Paul applies the passive voice verb translated "those who sleep," which displays God "putting them to sleep." Believers sleep (as used euphemistically) because Jesus died. The sting is taken out of death for Christians because Jesus experienced the wrath of God poured upon Him. Paul expresses this well in the following: "For He [God] made Him [Jesus] who knew no sin to be sin for us, that we might become the righteousness of God in Him" (2 Cor. 5:21). "In Jesus" can be taken with "those who sleep" or "will bring." These saints died being in Christ, which reveals a relationship with Jesus (see also 1 Cor. 15:18).

"For this we say to you by the word of the Lord, that we who are alive and remain until the coming of the Lord will by no means precede those who are asleep" (v. 15). Some commentators believe this refers to a previous statement of Jesus like Acts 20:35, where you have the words recorded of Jesus ("it is more blessed to give than to receive") but not found in the Gospels. Yet the Rapture is a mystery, which means a holy secret not known in the past but now revealed. Paul calls it such in 1 Corinthians 15:51: "behold, I tell you a mystery." Therefore this is a revelation given directly to Paul, equivalent to other "thus says the Lord" statements (Luke 22:61; Acts 11:16) and Old Testament "thus says the Lord" declarations.

"We" is emphatic in the words "we who are alive." Paul believes he could be living at the imminent return of Jesus for the church. Observe for the second time he uses "we" in 1 Thessalonians 4:17. John also thinks he could be among the living at the Rapture. He shares, "And now, little children, abide in Him, that when He appears, we may have confidence and not be ashamed before Him at His coming" (1 John 2:28).

For the third time in 1 Thessalonians Paul points to the "coming of the Lord" (2:19; 3:13) and will do so again (5:23). The apostle uses emphatic negation as displayed "by no means" voicing a strong negative that the Rapture of the living does not "precede those who are asleep." Paul seems to be addressing a concern of the Thessalonian saints. Perhaps they wonder if those who die before the Rapture are disadvantaged. Stated otherwise, they ponder if church-age saints who die prior to the imminent return of Jesus would lose out on certain rewards. Emphatically, he says no!

"For the Lord Himself will descend from heaven with a shout, with the voice of an archangel, and with the trumpet of God. And the dead in Christ will rise first" (v. 16). Paul validates the previous statement with "for," which could also be translated "because." A personal return of Jesus is promised to gather the saints, unlike the Second Coming of Jesus Christ when angels do the gathering (Mark 13:26–27). Various commentators view "a shout," "the voice of an archangel," and "the trumpet of God" as three ways referring to the victorious event, while others see shout as a single idea with "the voice of an archangel" linked by "and" to "the trumpet of God" to more fully explain the shout. Yet the former interpretation prevails, since each of the three are introduced by "with" and shows three distinct sounds.

"With a shout," which only appears here from the Greek New Testament, is used in secular language for soldiers shouting while charging the enemy, and rowers exhorting one another in their work.

Next, "with a voice of an archangel" most likely points to Michael, who is the only angel specifically called an archangel in the Bible (Jude 9); yet Daniel 10:13 seems to allude to other archangels. "The trumpet of God" is the third sound offered in conjunction with the blessed appearing of Jesus. First Corinthians 15:52 states, "For the trumpet will sound, and the dead will be raised incorruptible, and we shall be changed." Again, those church-age saints are not disadvantaged who sleep in the Lord, which is bolstered by Paul's words, "And the dead in Christ will rise first."

"Then we who are alive and remain shall be caught up together with them in the clouds to meet the Lord in the air. And thus we shall always be with the Lord" (v. 17). Paul encourages the Thessalonian believers that the dead in Christ will be raised and are not inferior to the living saints. The adverb of time "then" shows the timing after the dead in Christ are raised. Once again Paul uses the first-person plural "we," explaining that he lived in light of the Rapture; however, he knew he might die before the blessed hope (1 Cor. 6:14; Phil. 1:20; 2 Tim. 4:6–7). "Remain" points to the privileged generation who will not experience death and "shall be caught up," which is a term generally denoting *to seize upon forcibly* (Matt. 11:12). The apostle used the term of himself being caught up to the third heaven (2 Cor. 12:2, 4). "With them" directs us to the dead in Christ. The location of the gathering is "in the clouds." The diminutive noun occurs pointing to a small cloud. Similarly the word is used of the Transfiguration (Matt. 17:5; Mark 9:7; Luke 9:34), Jesus' ascension (Acts 1:9), and the Second Coming (Matt. 24:30; 26:64; Mark 13:26; 14:62).

This blessed event in the sky is "to meet the Lord in the air." Interestingly, the Lord comes from one direction (heaven) and the saints from another (the earth) for the meeting. The "air," which Greek term appears seven times in the Greek New Testament, equals the atmosphere (Acts 22:23; 1 Cor. 9:26; 14:9; Rev. 9:2; 16:17). Beautifully Paul pens, "And thus we shall always be with the Lord." On another note, the Rapture must happen before the Tribulation, because if it happens afterward, who would populate the millennial kingdom?

"Therefore comfort one another with these words" (v. 18) gives us the conclusion on Paul's teaching. The Greek construction translated "therefore" refers to a conclusion. Paul uses the present imperative "comfort" that means to keep on encouraging each other. The apostle deliberatively uses "one another" to show the importance of the body of Christ building up the individual members. The revelation imparted to Paul, as communicated by the expression "for this we say to you" and now closing "with these words," reminds us of the inherent power of God's Word to change lives.

Wow! The Rapture should spur us on to godly living. Let's expand our understanding of the Rapture through relationship.

THE FAMILY REUNION AT THE RAPTURE – R

A holy secret not known in the past but now revealed gives us the definition of a mystery. Following is Paul's introduction to the Rapture: "Behold, I tell you a mystery: We shall not all sleep, but we shall all be changed—in a moment, in the twinkling of an eye, at the last trumpet. For the trumpet will sound, and the dead will be raised incorruptible, and we shall be changed" (1 Cor. 15:51–52). The apostle writes to a church, which is also described as a mystery in Ephesians 3:3, and shares information that is never found in the Old Testament. My dear brother or sister, you have been given a precious teaching that saints under the old covenant never knew.

No one knows the timing of the Rapture; it is also called the imminent return of Jesus. Yet the Bible teaches that it will occur before the start of the Tribulation, as described in Revelation 6–19. John writes to seven churches located in Asia Minor. To each church he writes, "He who has an ear, let him hear what the Spirit says to the churches." So, every church equally should employ what another is commanded. Philadelphia, the church of *brotherly love*, receives this promise: "Because you have kept My command to persevere, I also will keep you from the hour of trial which shall come upon the whole world, to test those who dwell on the earth" (Rev. 3:10). "The hour of trial" points to the Tribulation, because it is a global test for the inhabitants of the earth. Jesus promises that not only the church of Philadelphia, but every church, would not enter that period of time!

We have seen that the Rapture is a mystery and that the Lord Jesus could return instantly. Moreover, there exists a present application stated by both Paul and John. The church of Jesus Christ receives the charge to lead holy lives with the Rapture as an incentive. Paul charges Titus, "looking for the blessed hope and glorious appearing of our great God and Savior Jesus Christ, who gave Himself for us, that He might redeem us from every lawless deed and purify for Himself His own special people, zealous for good works" (Titus 2:13–14). Not only does Paul call the Rapture "the blessed hope" but prescribes holy living in light of the event.

John's teaching concurs with Paul's instruction. "And now, little children," writes the apostle of love, "abide in Him, that when He appears, we may have confidence and not be ashamed before Him at His coming" (1 John 2:28). Currently children of the King are to keep in constant communion with the Lord by walking with Him. This will permit the believer to have *all speech* or *freedom of speech*, which is the literal meaning of "confidence," when Jesus makes a personal appearance for us.

I hope you are blessed by the brief tour of Rapture passages. Let's lace up our work boots to prepare for applying what we have learned.

THE FAMILY REUNION AT THE RAPTURE – E

Having a beloved Christian family member die causes us to grieve. Yet our grief should not imitate that of a lost world because they do not have the assurance of salvation like us. *Don't overly mourn the home-going of Christians* (vv. 13–14). Thankfully our salvation is secure through the promise of Jesus who cannot lie (John 10:28–29). Paul testifies that for the believer "to be absent from the body [is] to be present with the Lord" (2 Cor. 5:8). Therefore we should not mourn like the unsaved, who have no guarantees about the afterlife.

Jesus did mourn at the tomb of Lazarus (John 11:35). Yet He knew that offering His life to be a sacrifice for sin would provide a means whereby we could be born again. The One who is "the way, the truth, and the life" (John 14:6) enables us to have confidence that we will again see our Christian loved ones when we die or at the Rapture (should we survive until then). Take heart; *don't overly mourn the home-going of Christians.*

Do you have fond memories from a family reunion? The Rapture will provide the greatest family reunion ever. Not only will you see departed loved ones, but also discover how extensive is the family of God. *Living and dead Christians reunite at the Rapture* (vv. 15–17). The Rapture takes us instantly into the presence of Jesus and we will be fully conformed to His image. John expresses the wonder of it all, "Beloved, now we are children of God; and it has not yet been revealed what we shall be, but we know that when He is revealed, we shall be like Him, for we shall see Him as He is" (1 John 3:2).

Imagine the fullness of joy by just being with Jesus! Furthermore, consider what it will be like not having a sin nature and Satan to distract or tempt us. Then ponder how awesome the fellowship with the saints will be since we will be like our Lord and not have the old man tugging us in the wrong direction.

Be encouraged by the revealed Rapture mystery (v. 18). I love Paul's conclusion in our Rapture passage: "Therefore comfort one another with these words" (v. 18). The Thessalonian saints seemed to be confused about dying before the Rapture and perhaps missing out on certain rewards or benefits. Paul clearly shows that is not the case. Both departed Christian loved ones and those who are alive when Jesus returns receive equal treatment. Knowing that these words were written by Paul by inspiration of the Holy Spirit brought encouragement to the saints at Thessalonica; let us read them once again to build ourselves up in the faith:

> But I do not want you to be ignorant, brethren, concerning those who have fallen asleep, lest you sorrow as others

who have no hope. For if we believe that Jesus died and rose again, even so God will bring with Him those who sleep in Jesus.

For this we say to you by the word of the Lord, that we who are alive and remain until the coming of the Lord will by no means precede those who are asleep. For the Lord Himself will descend from heaven with a shout, with the voice of an archangel, and with the trumpet of God. And the dead in Christ will rise first. Then we who are alive and remain shall be caught up together with them in the clouds to meet the Lord in the air. And thus we shall always be with the Lord. Therefore comfort one another with these words.

CHAPTER TWELVE

WILL CHURCH-AGE SAINTS EXPERIENCE THE DAY OF THE LORD?

1 Thessalonians 5:1–11

A buddy and I were shooting hoops on one side of a full-length basketball court at the local park. Four older young men occupied the other court. They played basketball for a while and then privately huddled on the grass. Being ten years old and curious (nosy) led me to eavesdrop on their conversation. These less-than-exemplary youth talked in quiet tones about robbing a nearby house. Unfortunately I discovered several days later about a home being burglarized just down the street where I lived, not far from the basketball court.

In 1 Thessalonians 5:1–11 Paul speaks about a thief in the night (vv. 2, 4). The term he uses, "thief," refers to a sneak thief. Like these four juvenile delinquents who broke into an unoccupied home at night while no one was home, the day of the Lord will overtake the unsaved by stealth.

Let's prayerfully peruse the following two translations.

But concerning the times and the seasons, brethren, you have no need that I should write to you. For you yourselves know perfectly that the day of the Lord so comes as a thief in the night. For when they say, "Peace and safety!" then sudden destruction comes upon them, as labor pains upon a pregnant woman. And they shall not escape. But you, brethren, are not in darkness, so that this Day should overtake you as a thief. You are all sons of light and sons of the day. We are not of the night nor of darkness. Therefore let us not sleep, as others do, but let us watch and be sober. For those who sleep, sleep at night, and those who get drunk are drunk at night. But let us who are of the day be sober, putting on the breastplate of faith and love, and as a helmet the hope of salvation. For God did not appoint us to wrath, but to obtain salvation through our Lord Jesus Christ, who died for us, that whether we wake or sleep, we should live together with Him.

Therefore comfort each other and edify one another, just as you also are doing. (1 Thess. 5:1–11)

Now, brothers and sisters, about times and dates we do not need to write to you, for you know very well that the day of the Lord will come like a thief in the night. While people are saying, "Peace and safety," destruction will come on them suddenly, as labor pains on a pregnant woman, and they will not escape.

But you, brothers and sisters, are not in darkness so that this day should surprise you like a thief. You are all children of the light and children of the day. We do not belong to the night or to the darkness. So then, let us not be like others, who are asleep, but let us be awake and sober. For those who sleep, sleep at night, and those who get drunk, get drunk at night. But since we belong to the day, let us be sober, putting on faith and love as a breastplate, and the hope of salvation as a helmet. For God did not appoint us to suffer wrath but to receive salvation through our Lord Jesus Christ. He died for us so that, whether we are awake or asleep, we may live together with him. Therefore encourage one another and build each other up, just as in fact you are doing. (1 Thess. 5:1–11, NIV)

A Thief in the Night – F

- What do the words "but concerning" introduce (v. 1)?

- Why does Paul write, "the day of the Lord so comes as a thief in the night" (v. 2)?
- Who does Paul refer to as "they" and "them" (v. 3)?
- Are "sleep," "watch," and "be sober" used literally or metaphorically (v. 6)?
- How should the word "salvation" be understood in its context (vv. 8, 9)?
- What theological term best describes the words "who died for us" (v. 10)?
- What is the "therefore" there for in 1 Thessalonians 5:11?
- Can you identify the two commands (v. 11)?

A THIEF IN THE NIGHT – I

Paul often introduces a new topic by the words "but concerning" (1 Thess. 4:9; 1 Cor. 7:1; 8:1; 12:1; 16:1). He writes, "But concerning the times and the seasons, brethren, you have no need that I should write to you" (v. 1). "Times and seasons" appear together here and Acts 1:7 and speak of end-time events: Rapture, Day of the Lord (including the Tribulation and Millennium) and the New Jerusalem. *A period of duration* is the meaning of "times." Our English term "chronology" derives from the Greek. There is no exact equivalent to "seasons," but generally refers to *a season of time*. Inherent to the word is that of *opportunity* as in Galatians 6:10: "Therefore, as we have opportunity [translated "seasons" in 1 Thessalonians 5:1], let us do good to all, especially to those who are of the household of faith."

"Brethren" shows not only Paul's warmth as a pastor for these sheep but also displays a transition to another topic, as in 1 Thessalonians 4:13. Paul first uses a negative and then a positive to communicate the Thessalonians' comprehensive eschatological training. He writes negatively, "You have no need that I should write to you." The missionaries adequately schooled these saints concerning the last days while with them for a relatively short period of time.

Next, Paul gives the statement positively. He shares, "For you yourselves know perfectly that the day of the Lord so comes as a thief in the night" (v. 2). "For" gives the reason why Paul didn't need to write to the saints about the times and seasons. "You" in "you your-selves know" is placed emphatically, stressing the saints' knowledge. The adverb "perfectly," which emerges five times from the Greek New Testament, carries the meaning *to search out and investigate thoroughly.* Matthew uses it first of Herod sending the Magi to Bethlehem to "search carefully [translated "perfectly" in our text] for the Young Child" (Matt. 2:8). Doctor Luke applies the term to his thorough knowledge about Jesus from his research. He documents, "it seemed good to me also, having had perfect understanding of all things from the very first, to write to you an orderly account, most excellent Theophilus" (Luke 1:3).

We studied about the Rapture from the previous paragraph in 1 Thessalonians 4:13–18. Paul now explains about "the day of the Lord." From the Old Testament it deals with the Tribulation (as described in Revelation 6–19) and the New Testament extends the timeframe into the millennial kingdom (2 Pet. 3:10). Amos twice calls the Tribula-tion "darkness" and Isaiah labels it as "the day of vengeance of our God" (Isa. 61:2). He then writes, "for the day of vengeance is in My heart" (Isa. 63:4).

The expression "thief in the night" only occurs in the context of the day of the Lord (1 Thess. 5:2; 2 Pet. 3:10). This period of judgment will quickly come upon the unsaved because they are not expecting it.

"For when they say, 'Peace and safety!' then sudden destruction comes upon them, as labor pains upon a pregnant woman. And they shall not escape" (v. 3). Paul uses the present tense "say," showing a continual speaking. The continual chatter promises an inner "peace" and outer "safety," with its false promise of serenity and protection. *At that time,* which is the meaning of "then," when the people are led to believe all is secure emerges "sudden destruction." The adjective "sudden" communicates something *unexpected* and *not anticipated.*

Luke gives us the only other use of the term in Luke 21:34, which is translated "unexpectedly." He quotes Jesus, who says, "But take heed to yourselves, lest your hearts be weighed down with carousing, drunkenness, and cares of this life, and that Day come on you unexpectedly."

Although the unsaved are not anticipating the "destruction," it will arrive. *Ruination* is the meaning of the word "destruction." Paul first uses the term in 1 Corinthians 5:5 about a habitually sinning immoral man who is being excommunicated for his refusal to repent over his sin. The apostle commands, "deliver such a one to Satan for the destruction of the flesh, that his spirit may be saved in the day of the Lord Jesus." Rejecting Jesus leads to a "sudden destruction." It happens swiftly "as labor pains upon a pregnant woman"!

One thing is certain about those who embrace the false promise of "peace and safety," writes Paul: "And they shall not escape." We are told strongly (as the words "shall not" from the Greek show emphatic negation) that the unsaved will not "escape." Seven times the verb surfaces from the Greek New Testament, which literally conveys *to flee out*. Luke quoting Jesus gives us the first appearance, "Watch therefore, and pray always that you may be counted worthy to escape all these things that will come to pass, and to stand before the Son of Man" (Luke 21:36). The anonymous writer of Hebrews also uses the term, "how shall we escape if we neglect so great a salvation" (Heb. 2:3). Clearly the unsaved will not be able to flee from the Tribulation.

"But you, brethren," writes their spiritual father in 1 Thessalonians 5:4, "are not in darkness, so that this Day should overtake you as a thief." Paul places "you" emphatically at the beginning of the sentence and contrasts the saints with the unsaved ("them" and "they") in the previous verse. He once again reminds his brothers and sisters who they are in Jesus by addressing them as "brethren." Moreover, the redeemed saints "are not in darkness, so that this Day should overtake you as a thief." Thieves like the cover of darkness to ply their trade; these saints would not enter the Tribulation, but still need to be vigilant.

Again (v. 4) the "you" is emphatic in "you are all sons of light and sons of the day. We are not of the night nor of darkness" (v. 5). Also, the "all" is emphatically placed first in the Greek sentence. In another Rapture passage Paul reminds the Corinthian saints, "Behold, I tell you a mystery: We shall not all sleep, but we shall all be changed" (1 Cor. 15:51). Twice he reminds the Corinthians that "all" of them will be fully conformed to the image of Jesus. "We are not of the night nor of darkness," pens Paul, because "He has delivered us from the power of darkness and conveyed us into the kingdom of the Son of His love" (Col. 1:13).

Two Greek words give a conclusion, and then the author makes a negative statement followed by a positive one in 1 Thessalonians 5:6: "Therefore let us not sleep, as others do, but let us watch and be sober." The negative "not" precedes the present tense verb "sleep" that can be used of physical sleep (Matt. 8:24), but arises here to refer to spiritual indifference (Rom. 13:11–13; Eph. 5:14). Paul desires the saints at Thessalonica not to be like the unsaved ("as others do"), "but let us watch and be sober." Both verbs "watch" and "be sober" are in the present tense. Matthew records the first use of "watch" as given by Jesus, "watch therefore, for you do not know what hour your Lord is coming" (Matthew 24:42). *To be sober-minded* gives us the notion of "sober." Peter warns, "Be sober, be vigilant; because your adversary the devil walks about like a roaring lion, seeking whom he may devour" (1 Pet. 5:8).

"For those who sleep, sleep at night," warns Paul, "and those who get drunk get drunk at night" (v. 7). Paul's use of "for" confirms the previous statement. The apostle then either uses the terms "sleep" and "drunk," literally describing two activities that belong to night or metaphorically. The latter idea seems more likely as that is how the apostle employed "sleep" in 1 Thessalonians 5:6. Therefore "sleep" indicates a passive indifference (spiritually) and "drunk" to an aggressive sense of sinning.

Paul continues his metaphorical illustrations, "But let us who are of the day be sober, putting on the breastplate of faith and love, and as a helmet the hope of salvation" (v. 8). Both appearances of "sober" (vv. 6, 8) are in the present tense, showing a continual sober-mindedness. Dressing for battlefield success becomes the exhortation of the warrior Paul. "Putting on" is an ingressive aorist tense verb and expresses the beginning of an action. In Ephesians 6:11 Paul tells the saints, "Put on the whole armor of God."

Specifically Paul gives two items for the saints to wear: "the breastplate of faith and love, and as a helmet the hope of salvation." Breastplates consisted of two pieces; one protected the front and the other the back. They covered the body from the neck to the thighs. By "faith" God's children are protected by the breastplate, and their "love" for God motivates them not to sin (Matt. 22:37). The hope is in the direction of salvation (an objective genitive). It is built upon the historical facts of Jesus' death and resurrection and anticipates salvation's completion through glorification.

"For God did not appoint us to wrath, but to obtain salvation through our Lord Jesus Christ" (v. 9). Paul's "for" shows the reason why the saints should keep on their armor. The middle voice verb "appoint" communicates that God "did not appoint [for Himself] us to wrath." The Greek term "wrath" speaks of *a state of mind*. Children of the King are not appointed to the Tribulation, which is a period of wrath (Rev. 6:17), nor to eternal damnation (Rom. 5:9). Rather, God's sovereign plan *acquires*—which is the meaning of "obtain"— salvation for us through Jesus Christ.

Referring to Jesus, Paul writes, "who died for us, that whether we wake or sleep, we should live together with Him" (v. 10). Once again Paul shares a common theme of Jesus' substitutionary atonement (Rom. 5:6, 7, 8; 1 Thess. 4:14). The expression "that whether we wake or sleep" can possibly be seen as a physical paying attention and sleeping, but more likely as spiritually and morally being watchful and alert. Regardless of the church-age saints' spiritual condition, "we should live together with Him." Stated otherwise, all children of God will participate in the Rapture (1 Cor. 15:51–52).

Paul's use of the inferential conjunction "therefore" gives a conclusion based upon his previous argumentation: "Therefore comfort each other and edify one another, just as you also are doing" (v. 11). Both "comfort" and "edify" occur in the present tense and are imperatives. They are instructed to keep on doing what they have done in the past! Clearly the saints had modeled consistency, and the apostle encourages them to maintain that lifestyle of service.

Now that we've interpreted 1 Thessalonians 5:1–11, let's consider the implications of not being in the darkness.

A THIEF IN THE NIGHT – R

Do you remember when you walked in darkness in your lost state? Children of God can look back at their former condition and express their appreciation for being redeemed. Paul writes to those who have been delivered from bondage, "But you, brethren, are not in darkness, so that this Day should overtake you as a thief" (v. 4). The apostle's choice of term ("darkness") conveys having spiritual blinders on and being led by the prince of darkness, Satan.

Judas chooses to remain in darkness even after being with the Light of the World. Jesus washes his feet and that of the other apostles at the Passover. Yet Judas is determined to betray Jesus. After leaving the Passover meal, John records, "And it was night" (John 13:30). The imperfect tense shows continuous action in past time, revealing it was continually night. Perhaps John subtly shows that Judas would forever be in the darkness. Later Jesus calls him "the son of perdition" (John 17:12), which in the Hebrew construct form means that he is a son belonging to the category of perdition. Scripture had prophesied that Judas, a friend of the Lord, would betray Him (Ps. 41:9).

The Ephesian saints had a background of magical practices, being under the sway of Satan. Paul writes the following to those believers: "This I say, therefore, and testify in the Lord, that you should no longer walk as the rest of the Gentiles walk, in the futility of their mind, having their understanding darkened, being alienated from the life of

God, because of the ignorance that is in them, because of the blindness of their heart; who, being past feeling, have given themselves over to lewdness, to work all uncleanness with greediness" (Eph. 4:17–19). Paul then adds, "But you have not so learned Christ" (v. 20).

The devil and his minions have an ominous rule. Paul depicts the believer's struggle with his organized spiritual mafia: "For we do not wrestle against flesh and blood, but against principalities, against powers, against the rulers of the darkness of this age, against spiritual hosts of wickedness in the heavenly places" (Eph. 6:12). Appropriately, five times Paul uses "against," showing the current struggle between those in the light versus those in the darkness. Thankfully we have been transferred by the substitutionary atonement of Christ from one kingdom into another. To the Colossian saints Paul writes, "He has delivered us from the power of darkness and conveyed us into the kingdom of the Son of His love" (Col. 1:13).

Amos twice calls the Tribulation darkness (Amos 5:18, 20). We are to walk with the light of the world and thus let our light beam out. Jesus emphatically tells His followers, "You are the light of the world. A city that is set on a hill cannot be hidden. Nor do they light a lamp and put it under a basket, but on a lampstand, and it gives light to all who are in the house. Let your light so shine before men, that they may see your good works and glorify your Father in heaven" (Matt. 5:14–16). Let's bask in the light and shine for Jesus!

A THIEF IN THE NIGHT – E

The unsaved will not escape the Tribulation (vv. 1–3) states our first employment point. Paul experienced persecution at Thessalonica, as did those who believed on Jesus (Acts 17:1–10). Emphatically the apostle proclaims about the persecutors, "and they shall not escape" (1 Thess. 5:3). In Paul's second epistle he graphically describes the future judgment on the unjust. He writes, "since it is a righteous thing with God to repay with tribulation those who trouble you, and to give you who are troubled rest with us when the Lord Jesus is revealed from heaven with His mighty angels, in flaming fire taking vengeance on those who do not know God, and on those who do not obey the gospel of our Lord Jesus Christ. These shall be punished with everlasting destruction from the presence of the Lord and from the glory of His power" (2 Thess. 1:6–9).

Vengeance is not ours to take upon those who persecute the saints. Be reminded, "Beloved, do not avenge yourselves, but rather give place to wrath; for it is written, 'Vengeance is Mine, I will repay,' says the Lord" (Rom. 12:19). Ponder the outcome of those who deny God's Word and attack believers!

Darkness attempts to shut down the light. *Vigilantly walk with God as children of light* (vv. 4–10) is our second employment point. Satan and his ambassadors seek to influence children of the day. Abiding with the Lord keeps us in the realm of His light and presence, and away from the impurities of darkness. Your assignment, which is a lifetime mission, is to remain in the light. Paul commands the saints at Ephesus, "Walk as children of the light" (Eph. 5:8). Dedicate yourself to the Lord (Rom. 12:1–2) and commit to moment-by-moment abiding with the Lord.

Christians can easily get discouraged on their pilgrimage to heaven. At times the path is arduous and there are many bumps along the route. So, let's heed the following: *Continue to encourage and build up each other* (v. 11). After teaching on the differences of children of darkness versus sons of the light, he writes, "Therefore comfort each other and edify one another, just as you also are doing."

What is your plan to build up fellow believers? To begin with, develop a prayer list including Christians that you spend time with regularly. Ask the Lord to guide you how to be a blessing to different saints. He might direct you to send a note of encouragement, pray with one who is struggling, or lead you to encourage them in other ways. The point is to *continue to encourage and build up each other*. Paul makes great efforts to do so, and we should follow in his footsteps!

CHAPTER THIRTEEN

PRACTICAL EXHORTATIONS PROMOTING CHURCH GROWTH

1 Thessalonians 5:12–22

I am blessed with three adult sons and five grandchildren. When my sons were young, they regularly played with twin boys who lived on our street. My eldest son Joshua asked the fraternal twins about the vocation of their father. One responded, "He is a roofer." Then one of the twins asked Joshua, "What does your dad do for a living?"

He replied, "My dad doesn't have a job; he's a pastor." Needless to say, I had a private conversation to make a slight correction to Joshua's misinformed statement after his friends departed!

Paul seems to make a slight correction to the saints' thinking at Thessalonica who are not appreciating their pastors (1 Thess. 5:12–13). The apostle builds upon his previous statement in 1 Thessalonians 5:11 to "comfort each other and edify one another" with a series of practical exhortations. Prepare your hearts to reverently read 1 Thessalonians 5:12–22.

And we urge you, brethren, to recognize those who labor among you, and are over you in the Lord and admonish you, and to esteem them very highly in love for their work's sake. Be at peace among yourselves.

Now we exhort you, brethren, warn those who are unruly, comfort the fainthearted, uphold the weak, be patient with all. See that no one renders evil for evil to anyone, but always pursue what is good both for yourselves and for all.

Rejoice always, pray without ceasing, in everything give thanks; for this is the will of God in Christ Jesus for you.

Do not quench the Spirit. Do not despise prophecies. Test all things; hold fast what is good. Abstain from every form of evil. (1 Thess. 5:12–22)

My friends, we ask you to be thoughtful of your leaders who work hard and tell you how to live for the Lord. Show them great respect and love because of their work. Try to get along with each other. My friends, we beg you to warn anyone who isn't living right. Encourage anyone who feels left out, help all who are weak, and be patient with everyone. Don't be hateful to people, just because they are hateful to you. Rather, be good to each other and to everyone else.

Always be joyful and never stop praying. Whatever happens, keep thanking God because of Jesus Christ. This is what God wants you to do.

Don't turn away God's Spirit or ignore prophecies. Put everything to the test. Accept what is good and don't have anything to do with evil. (1 Thess. 5:12–22, CEV)

INSTRUCTION IN CHURCH HEALTH 101 – F

- What do the words "to recognize" mean (v. 12)?
- Why should church leaders be greatly valued (v. 13)?
- How do the words "be at peace among yourselves" fit with the context (v. 13)?
- Do you "rejoice always" (v. 16)?
- Do you "pray without ceasing" (v. 17)?
- Do you "in everything give thanks" (v. 18)?
- What is the connection between 1 Thessalonians 5:19 and 5:20?
- Does "every form of evil" mean "every appearance of evil" (v. 22)?

INSTRUCTION IN CHURCH HEALTH 101 – I

"And we urge you, brethren, to recognize those who labor among you, and are over you in the Lord and admonish you," writes Paul (v. 12). The apostle shifts the topic as shown by the conjunction "and," but builds upon the term "comfort" or "exhortation" (v. 11) with a series of exhortations. His use of "urge" displays a tender tone of an appeal, which is further shown by addressing them once again as "brethren."

The NASB perhaps best captures the essence of "to recognize" with the translation, "appreciate." Keep in mind that Paul regularly chose elders in each church (Acts 14:23). Imagine how the congregation would view the individuals considered peers now appointed to be elders. After all, Paul had just founded the church approximately six months earlier. Now these leaders are to be treated with the respect due their office. One article ("the") governs three participles: "labor," "over you," and "admonish." The plural "labor" reflects how each church had more than one elder/pastor as described in the New Testament (Acts 14:23; 20:17; Phil. 1:1; Titus 1:5). Pastors are to be hard workers. *To be fatigued, weary, and exhausted* describes the term "labor." Paul is a model elder. He writes, "For to this end we both labor and suffer reproach, because we trust in the living God, who is the Savior of all men, especially of those who believe" (1 Tim. 4:10). Moreover, pastors are worthy of generous pay for their diligent effort. "Let the elders who rule well be counted worthy of double honor [generous pay]," pens Paul, "especially those who labor in the word and doctrine" (1 Tim. 5:17).

The second participle "over you" literally means *before* and *to stand*. (We just saw it used in 1 Timothy 5:17.) Paul applies the term to elders (1 Tim. 3:4, 5) and deacons (1 Tim. 3:12). "Admonish" transmits *to place in the mind.* Its first New Testament use is spoken by Paul to the Ephesians elders, and recorded by Luke: "Therefore watch, and remember that for three years I did not cease to warn [admonish] everyone night and day with tears" (Acts 20:31). Pastors are to be honored for carrying out these three difficult tasks.

Based upon the elders faithfully discharging their roles, Paul teaches about the congregation's responsibility to the elders: "and to esteem them very highly in love for their work's sake. Be at peace among yourselves" (v. 13). Continually are the saints "to esteem" their elders. In other words, they are to respect and regard them "very highly," which is a compound superlative meaning *beyond all measure*. "Exceedingly abundantly" is how the exact form is translated in Ephesians 3:20, where the apostle writes, "Now to Him who is able to do exceedingly abundantly above all that we ask or think, according to the power that works in us."

"In love" the believers at Thessalonica are to regard, or respect beyond all measure, their pastors. That is, they are to display good will or benevolence as a determined act to the elders. Paul then commands, "Be at peace among yourselves." Elders and church members will experience peace when godly pastors are rightly honored.

Paul's tone to the saints intensifies after having made an appeal to friends with the words "we urge you" in 1 Thessalonians 5:12; he transitions to a series of imperatives (vv. 14–15). "Now we exhort you, brethren, warn those who are unruly, comfort the fainthearted, uphold the weak, be patient to all. See that no one renders evil for evil to anyone, but always pursue what is good both for yourselves and for all" (vv. 14–15). The apostle and associates *come alongside of* (the meaning of "exhort") and give six imperatives to the "brethren."

First on Paul's list of imperatives is "warn those who are unruly." We just examined the term "warn" as translated "admonish" in 1 Thessalonians 5:12. "Unruly" surfaces only here from the Greek New Testament; it has the alpha prefix, signaling *not* and comes from the root *to arrange*. Paul commands the saints to warn or admonish those refusing to arrange themselves properly according to the standards they have been taught. Outside of the Bible, the term is used of a soldier out of rank and an army that is disorganized. The verbal form appears of those who are idle.

Next, the ever-encouraging apostle commands, "comfort the fainthearted." *To speak toward* imparts the literal understanding of "comfort."

The saints are to comfort with soothing words the "fainthearted," which comes from two Greek words meaning *little-souled*. John first uses the term "comfort" in John 11:19 of "women around Martha and Mary, to comfort them concerning their brother." First Thessalonians 2:11 imparts one of the four uses of "comfort," where Paul reminds the saints how he, Silas, and Timothy spoke soothing words to them.

Command number three says, "Uphold the weak." *To securely hold* carries the notion of "uphold," which is manifested four times from the Greek. Jesus first uses the term in Matthew 6:24 and is translated "will be loyal." He teaches that no one can have two masters, "or else he will be loyal to the one and despise the other." Particularly, the saints receive the imperative to support the "weak." The term "weak" means *without strength* and can refer to lacking physical strength (1 Pet. 3:7) or moral and spiritual strength (1 Cor. 8:7, 10), and the latter thought is used here.

Paul's fourth command is to "be patient with all." *Long to wrath* gives us the meaning of "patient." Truly patience is a virtue, and the saints are commanded to practice applying it to all people. The apostle uses the same term in 1 Corinthians 13:4, saying, "love suffers long and is kind." We are even to display patience as we wait for Jesus. James writes, "Therefore be patient, brethren, until the coming of the Lord. See how the farmer waits for the precious fruit of the earth, waiting patiently for it until it receives the early and latter rain. You also be patient. Establish your hearts, for the coming of the Lord is at hand" (James 5:7–8).

"See that no one renders evil for evil" is the fifth imperative in the series. *Bad* or *externally worthless* bestows the meaning of the adjective "bad." The contrasting conjunction "but" shows how saints who are treated badly should respond: "pursue what is good both for yourselves and for all." The present imperative "pursue" refers negatively to *being persecuted* (Matt. 5:10, 11, 12), and positively of seeking after godliness (1 Tim. 6:11; 2 Tim. 2:22).

Paul then transmits three imperatives, all in the present tense. Interestingly, all three commands are preceded by modifiers: "always"

(v. 16), "without ceasing" (v. 17), and "in everything" (v. 18). So, from the Greek word order we have, "always rejoice, without ceasing pray, in everything give thanks; for this is the will of God in Christ Jesus for you" (vv. 16–18). We now have the shortest verse from the Greek New Testament, "rejoice always," which is long on demands. (We will pursue this verse in more detail under relationship.)

Without intermission relays the meaning of "without ceasing." Paul practices what he commands others. "For God is my witness," writes a dedicated prayer warrior, "whom I serve with my spirit in the gospel of His Son, that without ceasing I make mention of you always in my prayers" (Rom. 1:9). The man of God not only has a prayerful disposition but a heart of continual thanksgiving. As he tells these saints to pray, he writes, "For this reason we also thank God without ceasing, because when you received the word of God which you heard from us, you welcomed it not as the word of men, but as it is in truth, the word of God" (1 Thess. 2:13). These three succinct commands (vv. 16–18) are part of God's will. There is no article ("the") before "will of God," so the triad doesn't describe the Lord's will in its entirety.

Our section of Scripture comes to a close with five brief commands; two are stated negatively (vv. 19–20), and three are given positively (vv. 21–22). Each imperative appears in the present tense, which seems to imply to stop doing something. "Do not quench the Spirit" passes on the first command. "Quench" first surfaces in Matthew 12:20 of a literal *putting out* or *extinguishing* a "smoking flax." Here Paul applies the term metaphorically, since it is impossible to extinguish the Holy Spirit. The second negative command sheds light on the former: "Do not despise prophecies" (v. 20). Paul's term "despise" has an intensifier affixed to it (preposition) and the verbal root means *to bring to nothing*. Perhaps the second letter to the Thessalonians (2:1–2) gives us insight to the saints' hesitancy to accept prophecy since false messages abounded, but by saying no to the authoritative message had them extinguishing or quenching the Spirit.

Finally, let's look at the three positively stated commands. "Test all things; hold fast what is good," pens Paul, "Abstain from every form of evil" (vv. 21–22). *Examine, try,* and *approve* sets out for us the meaning of "test." First John 4:1 highlights the importance of discernment on the part of the believer. John writes, "Beloved, do not believe every spirit, but test the spirits, whether they are of God; because many false prophets have gone out into the world." Spiritual saints employ a discerning eye to all things. Paul relays, "But he who is spiritual judges all things, yet he himself is rightly judged by no one" (1 Cor. 2:15).

The second positive statement follows: "Hold fast what is good." Nineteen times "hold fast" comes into the New Testament from the Greek. Paul uses the verb *I have* prefixed by a preposition to strengthen the term. Believers are to "hold fast" to that which is *morally good,* which is the meaning of "good." Finally, we are to "abstain from every form of evil." God desires the saints to protect themselves from experiencing evil. "Form" should be understood in light of its secular use of *class* or *kind* and not, as translated by the King James Version, "all appearance of evil." Even Jesus ministered to winebibbers, harlots, and publicans. Could His presence among them been an "appearance of evil"? Yet Jesus never participated in any act of evil or wickedness. Clearly "every form of evil" better aligns with the text.

Now that we've interpreted the many above imperatives, let us consider the wide-ranging use of "rejoice always."

INSTRUCTION IN CHURCH HEALTH 101 – R

Why might the shortest verse from the Greek New Testament be the most difficult to constantly apply? Just fourteen Greek letters gives us the command, "rejoice always." Please keep in mind that the one who pens these words did exactly that. The book of Philippians is replete with references to joy. What is so amazing is that Paul repeatedly tells the saints at Philippi to be joyful—yet he writes from prison—and expresses a fullness of joy while under house arrest. Amazing! Clearly Paul does not let his circumstances be the driving force of his joy, but the Holy Spirit.

Drawing near to Jesus produces joy. Observe that the travelers from afar (called Magi from the Greek), who travel perhaps for almost two years, experience joy when being guided to the Toddler's side. Matthew describes, "When they saw the star, they rejoiced with exceedingly great joy. And when they had come into the house, they saw the young Child with Mary His mother, and fell down and worshiped Him" (Matt. 2:10–11).

Even the trial of persecution cannot rob the child of God from joy. Jesus says, "Rejoice and be exceedingly glad, for great is your reward in heaven, for so they persecuted the prophets who were before you" (Matt. 5:12). Experientially the Thessalonians saints know joy in the midst of persecution (1 Thess. 1:6). Leading someone to Jesus who repents of his sin is another trigger for joy. Jesus teaches about the shepherd pursuing the errant sheep, "And if he should find it, assuredly, I say to you, he rejoices more over that sheep than over the ninety-nine that did not go astray" (Matt. 18:13).

Pondering the implications of Jesus' resurrection results in manifested joy. The women who went to the tomb expecting to find a dead Jesus soon realize He is alive. Matthew documents their response, "So they went out quickly from the tomb with fear and great joy, and ran to bring His disciples word" (Matt. 28:8). As a pastor for more than thirty years there exists one thing that repeatedly brings joy to my heart: saints being obedient to the Bible. John explains, "I rejoiced greatly that I have found some of your children walking in truth, as we have received commandment from the Father" (2 John 4).

Praise be to God the Father, Son, and Holy Spirit for granting us the privilege to experience joy despite our circumstances! Now it is that time again to put into practice all that we've learned; let's go to work!

INSTRUCTION IN CHURCH HEALTH 101 – E

Appreciate and love your leaders and experience peace (vv. 12–13) is our first employment point. Make it your daily practice to pray for your pastor, verbally encourage him whenever the occasion arises to do so, and come up with a plan how to honor him. Be creative; the point is that when you honor your pastor you are being obedient to God! Next, *serve the saints and overcome evil with good* (vv. 14–15). We live in a wicked world that first hated Christ, and will treat us the same. Genuine love displays itself to the lost even when you are being unfairly treated. Determine not to return in kind the same unjust treatment you receive, but to respond with love. Paul reminds us, "love suffers long and is kind" (1 Cor. 13:4).

God's will consists of rejoicing, praying, and giving thanks. *Continually rejoice, pray, and give thanks to fulfill God's will* derives from 1 Thessalonians 5:16–18. Walking with God becomes the key to do the impossible: always rejoice, without interruption pray, and always give thanks. Do a spiritual inventory of your devotional life, and make any necessary corrections to keep yourself abiding in Jesus.

Stop rejecting the Spirit and Word while clinging to good (vv. 19–22) is our fourth employment point. The five imperatives given in this section of Scripture must be obeyed. Ask God to search your heart to reveal whether you are just a student of the Word or are both a hearer and doer! A head full of information that doesn't reach our hearts and hands becomes a habitation for prideful thinking. Paul warns about knowledge without application (1 Cor. 8:1). Purpose to revere the written and spoken (preached) Word!

CHAPTER FOURTEEN

PAUL'S PASTORAL WISH
FOR THE SAINTS

1 Thessalonians 5:23–28

A young man went to a church fellowship with both of his ears bright red. One of his friends asked him, "What did you do to your ears?"

"Terrible thing," said the fellow. "While I was ironing my shirt to come tonight the phone rang, and well, I picked up the iron instead of the phone."

"That's so gross," said the sympathetic friend, "but what happened to the other ear?"

"The same guy called back!"

Well, the apostle Paul is the repeat caller in 1 Thessalonians 5:23. He stresses the need for the saints to depend upon God for their sanctification (1 Thess. 5:23a) and calls back with the same message (1 Thess. 5:23b). Let's carefully read both translations of 1 Thessalonians 5:23–28.

Now may the God of peace Himself sanctify you completely; and may your whole spirit, soul, and body be preserved blameless at the coming of our Lord Jesus Christ.

He who calls you is faithful, who also will do it.

Brethren, pray for us.

Greet all the brethren with a holy kiss.

I charge you by the Lord that this epistle be read to all the holy brethren.

The grace of our Lord Jesus Christ be with you. Amen. (1 Thess. 5:23–28)

Now may the God of peace Himself sanctify you entirely; and may your spirit and soul and body be preserved complete, without blame at the coming of our Lord Jesus Christ. Faithful is He who calls you, and He also will bring it to pass.

Brethren, pray for us.

Greet all the brethren with a holy kiss. I adjure you by the Lord to have this letter read to all the brethren.

The grace of our Lord Jesus Christ be with you. (1 Thess. 5:23–28, NASB)

PAUL'S FAREWELL ADDRESS FOR NOW – F

- Why does Paul use the optative (wish) mood with the word "sanctify" (v. 23)?

- Does Paul regularly speak about "the God of peace" toward the end of his letters (v. 23)?

- What do the words "spirit, soul, and "body" mean in the context of sanctification (v. 23)?

- Who ultimately completes the process of sanctification (v. 24)?

- What is "a holy kiss" (v. 26)?

- Why does Paul "charge you by the Lord that this epistle be read to all the holy brethren" (v. 27)?

- Is it Paul's practice to close all his letters with the blessing of "grace" (v. 28)?

PAUL'S FAREWELL ADDRESS FOR NOW – I

In the final section of our epistle Paul appeals to the saints to depend upon God for their sanctification. It is a strong wish because he states and restates his desire in 1 Thessalonians 5:23: "Now may the God of peace Himself sanctify you completely; and may your whole spirit, soul, and body be preserved blameless at the coming of our Lord Jesus Christ." The apostle picks up from 1 Thessalonians 3:11–13 and 4:3–8 the theme of sanctification. He uses the optative mood, which expresses a wish. Paul's desire is for these set-apart saints to progress in sanctification until Jesus returns.

Only "the God of peace" can complete the process. Paul often uses the expression toward the end of a letter (Rom. 15:33; 16:20; 2 Cor. 13:11; Phil. 4:9). Literally the Greek text says that He is "the God of the peace." Beautifully "peace" describes the nature of God and Jesus who is "the Prince of Peace" (Isa. 9:6). Peace delineates God's character and the Thessalonian experience since the justified "have peace with God through our Lord Jesus Christ" (Rom. 5:1). Moreover, Paul writes about the Son, "He Himself is our peace" (Eph. 2:14).

"Himself" is placed first in 1 Thessalonians 5:23 to reinforce God's unique ability to sanctify. The adjective "completely," which derives from the compound *all* and *completion*, appears only here from the Greek New Testament. Paul states forcefully that the God of peace Himself will entirely bring to completion our sanctification.

Like the fellow picking up the iron because the caller rang twice, Paul is coming back for a second time: "and may your whole spirit, soul, and body be preserved blameless at the coming of our Lord Jesus Christ." He uses the adjective "whole." The compound term literally communicates *all* and *a part*. The idea of the term describes not lacking anything possessing all its parts. Greek scholars say the adjective "completely" refers to a mature Christian character qualitatively pointing to perfection and the second adjective "whole" to a quantitative spiritual development.

Before examining the meaning of "spirit, soul, and body," we will briefly consider both the dichotomous and trichotomous views. The former sees the spirit and soul for the similar immaterial substance arguing for two functions: relationship to God and the seat of personality including emotions. They believe the body and soul (or spirit) at times describes the complete man (Matt. 10:28; 1 Cor. 5:3). On the other hand the trichotomous views the immaterial man as spirit and soul substantially, not just functionally. Paul is often cited as holding their position since he makes distinction between the natural or soul-ish man (1 Cor. 2:14) and the spiritual (1 Cor. 2:15; 15:44).

Since the Greek shows "spirit, soul, and body" as three distinct entities clearly separated by a definite article ("the") before each term and two conjunctions ("and"), the trichotomous view seems prefer-able. Moreover, the writer of Hebrews makes a distinction between soul and spirit (Heb. 4:12).

Deliberately Paul places "spirit" before "soul and body." The "spirit" consists of the immaterial part enabling man to connect to God. Adam's human spirit enabled him to walk with God. After the fall believers need to be justified in order to have a relationship with the Lord. Paul writes, "The Spirit Himself bears witness with our spirit that we are children of God." Next, the "soul" is the seat of personality, enabling the individual to be aware of his body and physical surroundings. In other words, the soul produces a self-conscious life. Placed third, the "body" refers to a physical body made up of parts. Sadly, Greek cul-ture esteemed man's spirit, but despised the body. That philosophy is opposed to the teaching of the Bible (1 Cor. 6:19–20).

Paul employs another optative mood verb. "Be preserved" derives from the term "warden" or "guard" and communicates *to watch over* or *keep an eye on*. Luke utilizes the term in Acts 12:5 of Peter being kept watch over in prison and then in Acts 16:23 referring to the charge given to the Philippian jailor to guard Paul. "Blameless" liter-ally means *without fault*. The apostle along with Silas and Timothy displayed this lifestyle (1 Thess. 2:10) and now Paul desires them to do the same "at the coming of our Lord Jesus Christ." *Being present* gives us the meaning of the term translated "coming." Paul used the term consistently throughout 1 Thessalonians of the imminent return of Jesus (2:19; 3:13; 4:15).

Thankfully, sanctification's completion isn't dependent upon the saints. Paul teaches, "He who calls you is faithful, who also will do it"

(v. 24). While under house arrest he would later write, "being confident of this very thing, that He who has begun a good work in you will complete it until the day of Jesus Christ" (Phil. 1:6). *To be persuaded* gives us the meaning of "faithful." We can have confidence in the God who calls us. The present-tense participle "calls" shows a continual calling to sanctification (1 Thess. 2:12; 4:7). Not only does He call us, but "also will do it." Since God cannot lie, neither can He violate the promises in His Word!

"Brethren, pray for us" (v. 25) is the command Paul pens. Although this is the last time "brethren" is employed in 1 Thessalonians, it is the first time the term appears in the beginning of the verse, which makes it emphatic by position. Paul faithfully seeks the prayers of others (Rom. 15:30; Eph. 6:19; Phil. 1:19; Col. 4:3; 2 Thess. 3:1). Is this one of his keys to success?

His next imperative is as follows: "Greet all the brethren with a holy kiss" (v. 26). This was a customary greeting in Paul's day. Traditionally the men kissed the men on the cheek and the women other women. Since it is a "holy" kiss there existed nothing sensual. Today the handshake has largely replaced the custom, but the holy kiss is still practiced in different parts of the world. "Kiss" derives from the verb *to love* or *befriend*. Judas used this custom to identify Jesus (Luke 22:48). The words "one another" often appear with "kiss" (Rom. 16:16; 1 Cor. 16:20; 2 Cor. 13:12; 1 Pet. 5:14).

Paul wants to make sure that everyone hears this epistle. "I charge you by the Lord that this epistle be read to all the holy brethren," commands Paul (v. 27). "I charge" puts the believers under oath and implores the saints to swear (Mark 5:7; Acts 19:13). The implication is that God will judge them if they don't follow through. Also, some commentators believe that a faction in the church might lead to all not hearing, while others think the grave language points to this being Scripture and should be heard by all. "Be read" literally means *to know up*. The concept conveys to read aloud.

"The grace of our Lord Jesus Christ be with you. Amen" imparts the final verse in 1 Thessalonians (v. 28). Grace points to *God's* favor.

We will probe the depths of grace under relationship, as the apostle has much to communicate on this subject.

PAUL'S FAREWELL ADDRESS FOR NOW – R

One of Paul's favorite things to write about is "grace," which emerges 156 times from the Greek New Testament. Masterfully, the apostle begins each letter with the topic of grace and does the same at the ending. Like bookends that hold a valuable set of writings, God's favor meets us for salvation, walks with us throughout life, and stays by our side until the journey is complete. Grace, the marvelous favor of God, stems from the eternal Father who truly sheds His grace on thee.

Look at the beginning of Paul's letter to the Thessalonians. "Grace to you and peace from God our Father and the Lord Jesus Christ" (1 Thess. 1:1). We first met grace at our salvation. Paul declares, "For by grace you have been saved through faith, and that not of yourselves; it is the gift of God, not of works, lest anyone should boast" (Eph. 2:8–9). Having grace as a traveling companion throughout life is one of those remarkable gifts from the Lord.

Truly we have been saved in order to serve the Lord (Eph. 2:10). Yet grace doesn't abandon us during our service for God; rather, His favor divinely enables us to accomplish great things. Consider Paul's self-assessment, "But by the grace of God I am what I am, and His grace toward me was not in vain; but I labored more abundantly than they all, yet not I, but the grace of God which was with me" (1 Cor. 15:10). The apostle's labors derived not from self-sufficiency, but because he depended upon the Lord's grace to strengthen him.

Paul often turned to God for help and sought others to pray for him; it was his practice. Since our Lord possesses infinite grace because He is an eternal being, there flows from His very nature as much favor as He chooses to bestow. "Let us therefore come boldly to the throne of grace," pens the anonymous writer, "that we may obtain mercy and find grace to help in time of need" (Heb. 4:16). If you will, God's well of grace never runs dry!

As the apostle begins each of his epistles writing about grace, he ends each one similarly (Rom. 16:20, 24; 1 Cor. 16:23; 2 Cor. 13:14; Gal. 6:18; Eph. 6:24; Phil. 4:23; Col. 4:18; 1 Thess. 5:28; 2 Thess. 3:18; 1 Tim. 6:21; 2 Tim. 4:22; Titus 3:15; Phlm. 25). The great apostle, prophet, pastor, and missionary extends to others that which he also first received. "The grace of our Lord Jesus Christ be with you. Amen" (1 Thess. 5:28).

PAUL'S FAREWELL ADDRESS FOR NOW – E

Servants of God understand the arduous path of following in Jesus' steps. Perhaps for this reason Paul culminates several of his letters writing to others about the God of peace. *Depend upon the faithful God of peace to sanctify you* (vv. 23–24) is employment point number one. Personally, we need to have faith in the God whose peace fills our hearts; know that He will complete the good work of sanctification He has started in us.

Satan attempts to discourage us from pursuing holiness. One of his tools consists of planting discontentment in our lives. The veteran apostle understands the importance of not wanting what belongs to others (covetousness) but being satisfied with God's provision for our lives. Your assignment is to read Philippians 4:4–13. You are to focus upon cultivating a hunger for holiness while seeking to be content in life. Paul's advice is as follows: "The things which you learned and received and heard and saw in me, these do, and the God of peace will be with you" (Phil. 4:9). Allow the God of peace to permeate your heart with His presence.

Pray for pastors, greet the saints, and read the Word (vv. 25–27) is our second employment point. Mature Christian pastors understand the vital need for prayer support. Not only does the apostle command the saints to pray for the missionary team in 1 Thessalonians (5:25), but also in the second epistle. He instructs, "Brethren, pray for us, that the word of the Lord may run swiftly and be glorified, just as it is with you" (2 Thess. 3:1). Daily pray for your pastors that God would greatly use them to train others and reach the lost. Pastor Paul also does the work of an evangelist, which means he needs prayer for open doors. He guides the saints to do the following: "meanwhile praying also for us, that God would open to us a door for the word, to speak the mystery of Christ, for which I am also in chains, that I may make it manifest, as I ought to speak" (Col. 4:3–4).

Also, commit to greet the saints. Easily we can take for granted the privilege to have brothers and sisters in Christ. Choose to be more aware of your Christian context, and bless each brother and sister in the Lord that you meet with an appropriate greeting (1 Thess. 5:26). Moreover, value the Word of God by reading it daily. Hearing God's Word produces a stronger faith (Rom. 10:17), and reading it imparts a blessing. John writes, "Blessed is he who reads and those who hear the words of this prophecy, and keep those things which are written in it; for the time is near" (Rev. 1:3). Don't let the cares of this life keep you from daily partaking of the wonderful words of life!

Finally, *desire the saints to know God's grace* (v. 28), our third employment point. We have seen how Paul begins and ends his epistles with grace. Humanly speaking, our tendency is to depend upon self. How easy it is to go through an entire day without leaning upon the everlasting arms. Cultivating a life of prayer becomes essential to thriving upon God's grace. Peter beautifully reminds us of the need to "grow in the grace and knowledge of our Lord and Savior Jesus Christ" (2 Pet. 3:18).

2 THESSALONIANS

PART ONE

CONTINUING DESPITE PERSECUTION

2 Thessalonians 1

CHAPTER FIFTEEN

CONNECT OTHERS TO THE FATHER AND SON'S GRACE AND PEACE

2 Thessalonians 1:1–2

Shortly before the homegoing of John Newton (the former slave trader who penned "Amazing Grace"), a fellow servant of God came and had breakfast with him. Newton's sight was poor but the friend would read the Scripture before the meal. The Scripture read stated, "by the grace of God I am what I am" (1 Cor. 15:10).

After a period of silence Newton said, "I am not what I ought to be! How imperfect and deficient I am! I am not what I wish to be, although I abhor that which is evil and would cleave to the good! I am not what I hope to be, but soon I shall be out of mortality, and with it all sin and imperfection. Though I am not what I ought to be, nor what I wish to be, nor yet what I hope to be, I can truly say I am not what I once was: a slave to sin and Satan. I can heartily join with the apostle and acknowledge that by the grace of God I am what I am!"

Like 1 Thessalonians, 2 Thessalonians begins with grace (1:2) and ends with grace (3:18). Several months have elapsed since Paul writes the first epistle. He pens his first letter from Corinth (AD 50–51). Paul seems to be still there since he, Silas, and Timothy don't appear together again through the book of Acts. The saints will need grace to fix some of the problems that remain (work related in 2 Thessalonians 3:6–10), which is exacerbated by them receiving deceptive communication that they have missed the Rapture (2 Thess. 2:1–2). Also, they continue to be persecuted (2 Thess. 1:4–12).

So, let's prayerfully concentrate on the reading of 2 Thessalonians 1:1–2.

Paul, Silas and Timothy,

To the church of the Thessalonians in God our Father and the Lord Jesus Christ: Grace and peace to you from God the Father and the Lord Jesus Christ. (2 Thess. 1:1–2, NIV)

THE GRACE AND PEACE CONNECTION – F

- Why doesn't Paul have a title after his name (v. 1)?
- What is the difference between 1 Thessalonians 1:1 and 2 Thessalonians 1:1?
- Do you remember the definition of grace (v. 2)?
- Do you recall the Hebrew term for peace (v. 2)?
- What is the significance of the grace and peace coming "from God our Father and the Lord Jesus Christ" (v. 2)?

THE GRACE AND PEACE CONNECTION – I

Paul, the author, includes the missionary team in the introduction: "Paul, Silvanus, and Timothy, To the church of the Thessalonians in God our Father and the Lord Jesus Christ" (v. 1). The apostle Paul self-identifies as the author of 2 Thessalonians (1:1; 3:17). His signature (3:17) testifies to the letter being authentic. Early church fathers such as Polycarp, Ignatius, and Justin agree to Paul's authorship. Moreover, observe how Paul's name does not have a title (apostle, bondservant, or prisoner) affixed to it. The saints at Thessalonica must have accepted Paul's authority since only these two letters (1 and 2 Thessalonians) don't have a title after his name.

Paul includes Silvanus in the greeting; he is both a Jewish man and has a Roman name (Silas) and Roman citizenship (Acts 16:37). Luke identifies him as a prophet (Romans 15:32), a church leader (Acts 15:27) and possessing a good reputation (Acts 15:22). He traveled with the apostle and together was incarcerated at Philippi (Acts 16:19–34). Peter speaks highly of him and appropriates his talents as the amanuensis of 1 Peter. The apostle to the Jews (Peter) writes, "By Silvanus, our faithful brother as I consider him, I have written to you briefly, exhorting and testifying that this is the true grace of God in which you stand" (1 Pet. 5:12).

The holy trio includes Timothy. More than a decade later Paul would write two epistles addressed to "a true son in the faith" (1 Tim. 1:2), also calling him "a beloved son" (2 Tim. 1:2). This native of Lystra (Acts 16:1) had a believing Jewish grandmother and mother (2 Tim. 1:5). Not only did Timothy have a good reputation among believers (Acts 16:2), but he remained a vital servant of Christ and ministry partner with Paul until the end (2 Tim. 4:9–13).

Timothy's stellar character receives the following endorsement from Paul: "For I have no one like-minded, who will sincerely care for your state. For all seek their own, not the things which are of Christ Jesus. But you know his proven character, that as a son with his father he served with me in the gospel" (Phil. 2:20–22). His presence would remind the saints of Paul. To the Corinthians Paul writes, "For this reason I have sent Timothy to you, who is my beloved and faithful son in the Lord, who will remind you of my ways in Christ, as I teach everywhere in every church" (1 Cor. 4:17).

This epistle is addressed "to the church of the Thessalonians in God our Father and the Lord Jesus Christ." During Paul's second missionary journey he invaded enemy territory consisting of a population of 250,000 people; he successfully planted a church in this strategic location (Acts 17:4). Paul acted upon the faith of Jesus' promise to build His church (Matt. 16:18). These former idolaters (1 Thess. 1:9) are transferred to a new kingdom as indicated by the word "in." Now they are "in God our Father and the Lord Jesus Christ."

"God our Father" gives us the only difference between 1 Thessalonians 1:1 and 2 Thessalonians 1:1. When the Bible refers to "God the Father" (1 Thess. 1:1) it refers to His person, however, the wording "God our Father" (2 Thess. 1:1) speaks of the personal relationship we have with God. Moreover, the juxtaposition of "the Lord Jesus Christ" to "God our Father" shows the Son's full deity. In other words, Jesus is the second member of the Trinity.

Next, Paul gives his traditional greeting: "Grace to you and peace from God our Father and the Lord Jesus Christ" (v. 2). Like bookends, "grace" begins and ends Paul's first letter to these saints (1:1; 5:28). He does the same in Second Thessalonians (1:2; 3:18). The apostle Paul grasps the necessity for God's favor upon his life personally, and all those to whom he would serve!

Coupled with "grace" is "peace." Its Old Testament counterpart *shalom* means "wholeness, completeness, and soundness." The apostle desires the Lord to prosper the saints spiritually, physically, and emotionally. Like 1 Thessalonians the apostle extends peace to the saints (1:1) and then expresses that "the God of peace" would sanctify them completely (5:23).

The believers from Thessalonica first experience peace when God justified them through the person of Jesus Christ (Rom. 5:1). After all, referring to Jesus, "He Himself is our peace," writes Paul (Eph. 2:14). Like 2 Thessalonians 1:1, Jesus is linked to the Father by the conjunction "and," which shows His equality with the Father.

We have now completed the interpretation of the introduction to 2 Thessalonians. Let's consider the wider implications under relationship.

THE GRACE AND PEACE CONNECTION – R

Twice God is called "our Father" within the first two verses of 2 Thessalonians. Under the Old Covenant such a designation is rare. Consider Isaiah 63:16, "Doubtless You are our Father, though Abraham was ignorant of us, and Israel does not acknowledge us. You, O LORD, are our Father; our Redeemer from Everlasting is Your name." Yet the New Testament is replete with references to God as our Father, stressing the believer's personal relationship with Him.

Perhaps the best-known example is the Lord's Prayer. Jesus addresses the Father as follows: "Our Father in heaven, Hallowed be Your name" (Matt. 6:9). Jesus not only calls God "Father" (John 17:1), but teaches His followers to do the same. Emphasizing a personal relationship with His own Father, Jesus prays, "that they [His disciples] all may be one, as You, Father, are in Me, and I in You; that they also may be one in Us, that the world may believe that You sent Me" (John 17:21). The unity of the Father and Son becomes the model of how all saints are to intimately walk with the Father and Son and have communion with one another.

The book of Ephesians begins by teaching about our spiritual blessings from the Father through the Son (Eph. 1:3; 2:6). As his custom Paul then transitions from the position of the believer (1:1–3:21) to his practice (4:1–6:24). Interestingly, the apostle holds up the model of the Trinity as the ultimate illustration of unity for the body of Christ: "There is one body and one Spirit, just as you were called in one hope of your calling; one Lord, one faith, one baptism; one God and Father of all, who is above all, and through all, and in you all" (Eph. 4:4–6). The transcendent God is also the personal Father of all believers.

God's desire to walk with us goes back to Him strolling with Adam and Eve in the garden of Eden. Yet through Jesus Christ the relationship becomes more fully revealed. In practice let us draw near our God, thanking Him daily for the sacred opportunity to call Him *our Father.*

Touring the Holy Bible investigating one topic sheds much light on the depth of our Father. It is that time again to apply what we've learned.

THE GRACE AND PEACE CONNECTION – E

We've investigated how *our Father* desires His children to stay close to Him. He has made this possible through the sacrifice of Jesus on our behalf. *Extend grace and peace through the Father and Son* (vv. 1–2) is our employment point. Question: How are you planning to extend God's grace and peace to the world? Have you considered a strategy to do this? Thankfully, there exists a biblical precedent to follow. We will consider the words and works of Jesus and Paul in this matter.

Our victorious Lord not only conquers death but also maps out a path for all believers to follow. He declares, "All authority has been given to Me in heaven and on earth. Go therefore and make disciples of all the nations, baptizing them in the name of the Father and of the Son and of the Holy Spirit, teaching them to observe all things that I have commanded you; and lo, I am with you always, even to the end of the age" (Matt. 28:18–20). "Make disciples" gives us the main verb and the following three participles modify the command: Go, baptize, and teach. In other words, Jesus' followers are to lead people to Christ both locally and globally, baptize them in the name of the Father, Son, and Holy Spirit, and instruct them in the ways of the Lord through the Word of God.

Jesus determined that He would not leave His disciples orphaned, so He dispatched the Holy Spirit to equip them to carry out His mission (John 14:16–18). Our Lord amplifies the teaching of John 14 in the book of Acts: "But you shall receive power when the Holy Spirit has come upon you; and you shall be witnesses to Me in Jerusalem, and in all Judea and Samaria, and to the end of the earth" (Acts 1:8). In essence, the apprentices of Jesus are to extend grace and peace to the world through the proclamation of the gospel.

As an obedient apostle, Paul has a strategy to spread God's grace and peace through Jesus: "And so I have made it my aim to preach the gospel, not where Christ was named, lest I should build upon another man's foundation" (Rom. 15:20). The determined apostle, knowing the Great Commission and that he is equipped by the indwelling Holy Spirit, charts a course to extend grace and peace to those who have never heard the gospel. No wonder why the Lord blessed him so much!

Now it's your turn to develop a plan to extend the grace and peace of the Father and Son to a lost world. To begin, ask the Lord for wisdom; then fast and pray to know your part in carrying out this most important work of the Lord.

CHAPTER SIXTEEN

JESUS' REVELATION TO REPAY THE WICKED AND REWARD THE RIGHTEOUS

2 Thessalonians 1:3–12

John Willard Peterson (November 1, 1921 – September 20, 2006) majorly impacted the Christian world from the 1950s through the 1970s with his music. Yet when he wrote lyrics early on there were challenging times.

Peterson had written "Over the Sunset Mountains" after contemplating the marvelous day when the saints enter heaven and see their Savior. The editor of music he approached was pleased with his song, but made the following suggestion: "Take out the name Jesus and focus a bit more on heaven." Peterson thought, "Heaven without Jesus? That is unthinkable." So he picked up his manuscript and left.

Clearly Paul is pleased that the saints at Thessalonica will be with Jesus in heaven, but also expresses the affliction of wrath upon those rejecting Him.

How privileged we are to read God's Word. Let's focus attentively to the two translations of 2 Thessalonians 1:3–12.

We are bound to thank God always for you, brethren, as it is fitting, because your faith grows exceedingly, and the love of every one of you all abounds toward each other, so that we ourselves boast of you among the churches of God for your patience and faith in all your persecutions and tribulations that you endure, which is manifest evidence of the righteous judgment of God, that you may be counted worthy of the kingdom of God, for which you also suffer; since it is a righteous thing with God to repay with tribulation those who trouble you, and to give you who are troubled rest with us when the Lord Jesus is revealed from heaven with His mighty angels, in flaming fire taking vengeance on those who do not know God, and on those who do not obey the gospel of our Lord Jesus Christ. These shall be punished with everlasting destruction from the presence of the Lord and from the glory of His power, when He comes, in that Day, to be glorified in His saints and to be admired among all those who believe, because our testimony among you was believed.

Therefore we also pray always for you that our God would count you worthy of this calling, and fulfill all the good pleasure of His goodness and the work of faith with power, that the name of our Lord Jesus Christ may be glorified in you, and you in Him, according to the grace of our God and the Lord Jesus Christ. (2 Thess. 1:3–12)

My dear friends, we always have good reason to thank God for you, because your faith in God and your love for each other keep growing all the time. That's why we brag about you to all of God's churches. We tell them how patient you are and how you keep on having faith, even though you are going through a lot of trouble and suffering.

All of this shows that God judges fairly and that he is making you fit to share in his kingdom for which you are suffering. It is only right for God to punish everyone who is causing you trouble, but he will give you relief from your troubles. He will do the same for us, when the Lord Jesus comes from heaven with his powerful angels and with a flaming fire.

Our Lord Jesus will punish anyone who doesn't know God and won't obey his message. Their punishment will be eternal destruction, and they will be kept far from the presence of our Lord and his glorious strength. This will happen on that day when the Lord returns to be praised and honored by all who have faith in him and belong to him. This includes you, because you believed what we said.

God chose you, and we keep praying that God will make you worthy of being his people. We pray for God's power to help you do all the good things that you hope to do and that your faith makes you want to do. Then, because God and our Lord Jesus Christ are so kind, you will bring honor to the name of our Lord Jesus, and he will bring honor to you. (2 Thess. 1:3–12, CEV)

JESUS' SECOND COMING PAYMENT PLAN – F

- Why are Paul, Silas, and Timothy "bound to thank God" (v. 3)?
- What is missing in 2 Thessalonians when you compare 1 Thessalonians 1:3 with 2 Thessalonians 1:3–4?
- Why are the saints "counted worthy of the kingdom of God" (v. 5)?
- How will the wicked be repaid for afflicting the saints (v. 6)?
- What is God's reward for the persecuted believer (v. 7)?
- Are there two groups specified for judgment (v. 8)?
- Does "in that Day" refer to the Rapture or Second Coming (v. 10)?
- How do Paul, Silas, and Timothy pray for the Thessalonian saints (v. 11)?
- What is the purpose of Paul's prayer (v. 12)?

JESUS' SECOND COMING PAYMENT PLAN – I

From a heart full of gratitude Paul, Silas, and Timothy express an indebtedness to praise the Lord for the saints at Thessalonica. "We are bound to thank God always for you, brethren," writes Paul to those whom he dearly loves, "as it is fitting, because your faith grows exceedingly, and the love of every one of you all abounds toward each other" (v. 3). Paul's use of the present tense verb "we are bound" shows the leaders' continual obligation to thank the Lord for them. As a man in debt to another (like the servant in Matthew 18:28, where the verb first appears in the New Testament), Paul feels compelled to offer thanksgiving.

The apostle Paul doesn't give thanks in every epistle for the saints, and the absence of such in Galatians most likely reflects his disappointment in their lives. Yet he gives thanks "always" for these believers to God (1 Thess. 1:2; 2 Thess. 1:3). He calls the thanksgiving "fitting," which could also be translated "worthy." This term speaks of its inner or intrinsic value whereas another adjective translated "precious" or "honorable" (Greek *timios*) refers to its attributed value (1 Cor. 3:12; Heb. 13:4; Rev. 17:4; 18:12, 16; 21:11, 19).

Paul gives the cause of the thanksgiving to God: "because your faith grows exceedingly, and the love of every one of you all abounds toward each other." Graciously the Lord answers the prayers of Paul, Silas, and Timothy for the saints' faith to mature (1 Thess. 3:10). It "grows exceedingly," which term derives from a preposition that means *beyond* or used as an intensifier, and *to increase*. Although this word only appears here from the Greek New Testament, elsewhere Paul employs the prefix (preposition) with another verb, revealing that the Lord can answer prayers "exceedingly abundantly" above our expectation (Eph. 3:20).

Not only did Paul pray for the saints to mature in faith but also to increase in love (1 Thess. 3:12). It did! Their sacrificial love is now *more than enough*, which is the meaning of "abounds." Believers are to "do good to all, especially to those who are of the household of faith" (Gal. 6:10). The focus upon "one another" receives great attention from Paul to these saints (1 Thess. 3:12; 4:9, 18; 5:11, 15; 2 Thess. 1:3).

The result of the Thessalonian believers maturing in faith and love is given in 2 Thessalonians 1:4: "so that we ourselves boast of you among the churches of God for your patience and faith in all your persecutions and tribulations that you endure." Paul places their "patience and faith" under one article. "Patience" derives from the Greek meaning *steadfast endurance*, and "faith" can either point to their trust in the Lord or faithfulness as the term is used in Galatians 5:22 and Titus 2:10. In the midst of their "persecutions and tribulations" they remained loyal to the Lord, displaying their genuine salvation.

The vast majority of commentators don't consider the omission of "hope" in 1 Thessalonians 1:3 significant. They argue that since the saints at Thessalonica exhibit "patience" and "endure" their afflictions, the term "hope" is unnecessary. Yet 2 Thessalonians 2:1–2 shows that the believers through deceptive miscommunication thought they had missed the Rapture and entered the Tribulation. Personally, I believe the absence of the term "hope" in 2 Thessalonians 1:3–4 deliberately communicates that a key element for the thriving of the saints is now missing. After all, Paul calls the Rapture the "one hope of your calling" in Ephesians 4:4, and "the blessed hope" in Titus 2:13. Although the church continued to grow in Jesus, they are missing a vital unit for growth (1 Cor. 13:13).

Paul connects the "manifest evidence" of 2 Thessalonians 1:5 with the previous verse. He writes, "which is manifest evidence of the righteous judgment of God, that you may be counted worthy of the kingdom of God, for which you also suffer" (v. 5). The *hapax legomenon* (term only used once in the Greek New Testament) "manifest evidence" means *to show*. At the end of the noun Paul attaches an ending (*ma* from the Greek) communicating the result accomplished. Their steadfast enduring (v. 4) is evident for all to see.

"The righteous judgment of God" will be unleashed at Jesus' Second Coming. Paul shows the purpose of His just judgment "that you may be counted worthy of the kingdom of God." He applies an intensifier to the verb "worthy" to express that enduring strong suffering and persecution displays the genuineness of their faith and a total worthiness of the saint to enter God's kingdom.

Luke uses the same term in Acts 5:41 concerning the apostles being persecuted for Jesus. He pens after their release that they were "rejoicing that they were counted worthy to suffer shame for His name." The same author captures Paul's words in Acts 14:22: "We must through many tribulations enter the kingdom of God." While under house arrest the apostle Paul states to the saints at Philippi, "For to you it has been granted on behalf of Christ, not only to believe in Him, but also suffer for His name's sake" (Phil. 1:29). Children of God display their worthiness of God's kingdom when they identify with Jesus who first suffered for us!

Next, Paul uses an intensified form of the first-class condition "if," which is translated "since," and assumes the statement to be true. "Since it is a righteous thing with God to repay with tribulation those who trouble you" (v. 6). God's actions are appropriate. John records in the context of the Tribulation, "true and righteous are Your judgments" (Rev. 16:7). *To pay back* gives us the idea of the past tense infinitive "to repay." Earlier Paul employs the term positively: "for what thanks we can render" (1 Thess. 3:9). Here the term conveys a payment "with tribulation [for] those who trouble you." Paul shows the sowing and reaping process. In essence, those who pressured God's children through persecution would be afflicted with His righteous judgment.

The other side of the coin is now displayed concerning the righteousness of God. Paul continues, "and to give you who are troubled rest with us when the Lord Jesus is revealed from heaven with His mighty angels" (v. 7). Like the slackening of the bowstring, "rest" shows a relief from tension. It is also translated "liberty" (Acts 24:23). Paul does not refer to the Rapture by the words "when the Lord Jesus is revealed" since there is no judgment associated with the Rapture (1 Thess. 4:13–18); he directs us to the Second Coming of Jesus at the end of the Tribulation (Rev. 19:11–21). The term "revealed" occurs eighteen times from the Greek New Testament and its last use is found in Revelation 1:1, which anticipates Jesus' Second Coming.

Three prepositional phrases follow "when the Lord Jesus is revealed." The first is "from heaven." The One "who is seated at the right hand of the throne of the Majesty in the heavens" (Heb. 8:1) will return from that location "with His mighty angels," which is the second prepositional phrase. Jesus says, "For the Son of Man will come in the glory of His Father with His angels" (Matt. 16:27) and "When the Son of man comes in His glory, and all the holy angels with Him" (Matt. 25:31).

The third preposition phrase occurs in 2 Thessalonians 1:8: "in flaming fire taking vengeance on those who do not know God, and on those who do not obey the gospel of our Lord Jesus Christ." There exists debate if "in flaming fire" describes the person of the Lord or the means of judgment upon the ungodly. God's holy essence can be described by fire (Ex. 3:2; 19:18; Dan. 7:9–10). Yet if "in flaming fire" looks forward, then it refers to a fire of judgment (Matt. 3:12; 13:40, 42, 50). Either way, the following describes our Lord and actions: "For our God is a consuming fire" (Heb. 12:29).

Jesus will enact judgment upon two groups of people. Paul employs the definite article ("the") before each group, showing separateness. "On those who do not know God" possibly alludes to Jeremiah 10:25. "Pour out Your fury on the Gentiles," which gives the first group, "who do not know You." In 1 Thessalonians 4:5 Paul writes, "not in passion of lust, like the Gentiles who do not know You." A reference to the Jews follows in Paul's words: "and on those who do not obey the gospel of our Lord Jesus Christ." Speaking about the Jews, Paul writes, "But they have not all obeyed the gospel" (Rom. 10:16). No unbeliever, whether Gentile or Jew, will evade God's wrath during the Tribulation.

"These shall be punished with everlasting destruction from the presence of the Lord and from the glory of His power" (v. 9). The relative pronoun "these" connects the above two groups. "Shall be punished" translates two terms found together only here in the New Testament, carrying the notion that the judgment is just.

Then Paul gives the appositional phrase "with everlasting destruction." This judgment is expanded upon by two prepositional phrases, both showing separation as indicated by the preposition "from." First, the "everlasting destruction," not annihilation, is "from the presence of the Lord." Jesus describes eternal life as knowing both the Father and Son intimately (John 17:3). Eternal destruction consists of not knowing the Father and Son by being perpetually distanced from the true God. Secondly, "and from the glory of His power" again emphasizing being forever apart from the Lord. Paul's desire is to personally and intimately know the Lord and the power of His resurrection (Phil. 3:10). The unsaved are eternally banished from His glorious presence and power.

Jesus will return; the question is not if but when. Paul expounds, "When He comes, in that Day, to be glorified in His saints and to be admired among all those who believe, because our testimony among you was believed" (v. 10). Amazingly the apostle, in the Greek, writes "comes" in the past tense. In other words, Jesus' coming is so sure that Paul uses past time to describe a future event. "In the Day" does not refer to the Rapture but the Second Coming. Paul directs the readers to the Day of the Lord, which pertains to the Tribulation period.

The purpose of His return, as shown by the infinitive of purpose is "to be glorified" by His holy followers. Paul likely expresses that Jesus will return not just to be glorified "among" the saints but "in" the saints. His choice of preposition (here translated "among") normally comes into the English language as "in." The preposition "in" not only appears before "His saints" but also is affixed to the term "glorified," showing an inner transformation.

Jesus will also "be admired among all those who believe." *To marvel* grants us the meaning of "admired." The saints will be glorified by the Lord and simultaneously marvel at Him "because our testimony among you was believed." Emphatically Paul places "was believed" in the Greek. First Thessalonians 2:13 characterizes how the Thessalonians "received the word of God . . . as it is in truth, the word of God, which also effectively works in you who believe."

"Therefore we also pray always for you that our God would count you worthy of this calling, and fulfill all the good pleasure of His goodness and the work of faith with power" (v. 11). The Greek construction translated "therefore" closely links the following prayer

(vv. 11–12) with the previous section (vv. 5–10). Paul is a practitioner of what he preaches. Earlier he commands these saints to "pray without ceasing" (1 Thess. 5:17). This also characterizes his prayer life for the saints.

His purpose in praying, "that our God would count you worthy of this calling." By way of contrast, the centurion didn't consider himself worthy to visit Jesus. He humbly tells the Lord, "Therefore I did not even think myself worthy to come to You. But say the word, and my servant will be healed" (Luke 7:7). Suffering and persecution are difficult to spiritually and physically digest. Yet these are part and parcel "of this calling," which refers to the effectual call to salvation that is obeyed (see 2 Timothy 1:9 and Hebrews 3:1 for other examples).

Moreover, the saints are to "fulfill all the good pleasure of His goodness and the work of faith with power." *To be well pleasing* imparts the meaning of "good pleasure." Paul writes, "for it is God who works in you both to will and to do for His good pleasure" (Phil. 2:13). "His goodness" should lead to our practicing of goodness (Rom. 15:14; Gal. 5:22) "and the work of faith," which communicates the work that faith produces "with power." Only through God's ability can these things be done!

Paul gives his purpose as he prays: "that the name of our Lord Jesus Christ may be glorified in you, and you in Him, according to the grace of our God and the Lord Jesus Christ" (v. 12). To the Hebrew mind "the name" represent the person. Jesus carries the name (person) that saves the soul through faith (John 1:12; Acts 4:12). Paul hints at the mutual abiding of John 15 when he writes, "Jesus Christ may be gloried in you and you in Him." Not surprisingly this is "according to the grace of our God and the Lord Jesus Christ."

JESUS' SECOND COMING PAYMENT PLAN – R

The book of Revelation, like none other, describes the revelation of Jesus Christ and His Second Coming. He Himself is the One who does the unveiling throughout the entire final book of the Bible. John is stationed on the Isle of Patmos to record these things. We are given a threefold outline in Revelation 1:19. Jesus commands the apostle John, "Write the things which you have seen, and the things which are, and the things which will take place after this." Jesus takes us on a tour of three times zones: past (Rev. 1), present (Rev. 2–3), and future (Rev. 4).

After taking us to the throne room of God for a sneak peek at what happens in heaven prior to the Tribulation (Rev. 4–5), the seven-year period begins in Revelation 6. There are three waves, and each consists of seven judgments beginning with the seals, moving to the trumpets, and finally the bowls (Rev. 6–19). Half the world's population is destroyed by the mid–point of the Tribulation (Rev. 6:8; 9:18).

The second half of the Tribulation begins in Revelation 12. Satan is expelled from heaven and intensifies his persecution of the saints since he understands "that he has a short time" (Rev. 12:12). Jeremiah labels this period as "the time of Jacob's [Israel's] trouble" (Jer. 30:7). Jesus simply calls it "the great tribulation" (Matt. 24:21). Moreover, He says, "And unless those days were shortened, no flesh would be saved" (Matt. 24:22). In other words, the Great Tribulation could only last for this period of time, lest the entire world's population be depleted.

John gives us the theme of the book of Revelation in Revelation 1:7: "Behold, He is coming with clouds, and every eye will see Him." Jesus will return a second time at the end of the Tribulation. Revelation 19:11–21 gives us the details of His return. His conquest to destroy those gathered at Armageddon begins in Bozrah, Edom (Isaiah 63:1–5), and He will slay His enemies moving in a northerly direction until He touches down on the Mount of Olives (Zech. 14:1–4). Subsequently He will establish His kingdom on earth (Rev. 20).

Church-age saints can thank the Lord that we will be delivered in the Rapture prior to the Tribulation. The Tribulation is called a period of wrath (Rev. 6:17), and we have not been designated to experience His wrath (1 Thess. 1:10; 5:9). Praise God for the life, death, burial, and resurrection of the sinless Son of God. Believing on Him delivers us from the wrath of the Tribulation and eternal damnation (Rom. 5:9).

It is time again to apply what we have studied in 2 Thessalonians 1:3–12.

JESUS' SECOND COMING PAYMENT PLAN – E

Praise God for maturing suffering saints and honor them (vv. 3–4) gives us employment point number one. Paul seizes upon the opportunity to encourage the saints at Thessalonica for their maturation in the midst of persecution. He chooses not to be disingenuous and praise an unworthy church; this is why there lacks the giving of thanks for the saints of Galatia. On the other hand, he quickly lavishes praise upon these saints and thanksgiving to God for their spiritual growth while suffering.

Do you know a believer who is either being persecuted or suffering for his faith and maturing in spite of opposition? If so, take time and thank God for that individual. Likewise encourage this saint through a telephone call, text, email, or in person. Share how their maturity in the face of opposition has encouraged you personally.

Those who treat the saints with contempt will answer for their ungodly actions. *Anticipate God repaying the wicked and rewarding the righteous* (vv. 5–10) is our second employment point. Remarkably, our Lord keeps a perfect ledger. He knows the motives and wicked practices of those who persecute the saints and will recompense them accordingly. So, commit all vengeance to Him, and know He will act (Rom. 12:19). Likewise, look for your future reward directly from Jesus (2 Cor. 5:10). Every deed done for God's glory and sacrifice made will be recompensed; therefore, live with that guaranteed hope before you!

We know as Christians that we are called to be people of prayer. Yet how should we pray for believers who are being openly condemned and abused for serving the King of Kings? *Pray for believers to fulfill their calling and glorify Jesus* (vv. 11–12) is our third and final employment point for the passage before us. Whether an individual Christian suffers at the hands of the unjust or not, he has a calling to make disciples of the nations. Humbly ask the Lord to complete the good work He has started in that individual, and furthermore know that he will glorify Jesus when fulfilling his God-given mission.

PART TWO

CLARIFYING THE DAY OF CHRIST

2 Thessalonians 2

CHAPTER SEVENTEEN

THE RAPTURE, RESTRAINER, AND REIGNING ANTICHRIST

2 Thessalonians 2:1–12

The Roman emperor Gaius (Caligula) began to reign in AD 37. He attempted to place his own image (an idol) in the temple at Jerusalem according to Flavius Josephus; however, he was thwarted from completing his mission. Likewise, Antiochus IV (215–164 BC) erected an altar to Zeus in the temple, which led to the Maccabean revolt. Both of these ungodly men were considered to be the Antichrist by a group of their peers.

Our text does not look at those suspected of being the Antichrist from the past, but at the future Antichrist as described in the Bible. Here are some questions to consider before unpacking the riches of 2 Thessalonians 2:1–12: What consequences emerge from misunderstanding biblical eschatology? Also, what is keeping the Antichrist from currently dominating much of the world? Finally, what will put an end to the Antichrist's quest for world rulership?

Now, brethren, concerning the coming of our Lord Jesus Christ and our gathering together to Him, we ask you, not to be soon shaken in mind or troubled, either by spirit or by word or by letter, as if from us, as though the day of Christ had come. Let no one deceive you by any means; for that Day will not come unless the falling away comes first, and the man of sin is revealed, the son of perdition, who opposes and exalts himself above all that is called God or that is worshiped, so that he sits as God in the temple of God, showing himself that he is God.

Do you not remember that when I was still with you I told you these things? And now you know what is restraining, that he may be revealed in his own time. For the mystery of lawlessness is already at work; only He who now restrains will do so until He is taken out of the way. And then the lawless one will be revealed, whom the Lord will consume with the breath of His mouth and destroy with the brightness of His coming. The coming of the lawless one is according to the working of Satan, with all power; signs, and lying wonders,

and with all unrighteous deception among those who perish, because they did not receive the love of the truth, that they might be saved. And for this reason God will send them strong delusion, that they should believe the lie, that they all may be condemned who did not believe the truth but had pleasure in unrighteousness. (2 Thess. 2:1–12)

Now we request you, brethren, with regard to the coming of our Lord Jesus Christ and our gathering together to Him, that you not be quickly shaken from your composure or be disturbed either by a spirit or a message or a letter as if from us, to the effect that the day of the Lord has come. Let no one in any way deceive you, for it will not come unless the apostasy comes first, and the man of lawlessness is revealed, the son of destruction, who opposes and exalts himself above every so–called god or object of worship, so that he takes his seat in the temple of God, displaying himself as being God. Do you not remember that while I was still with you, I was telling you these things? And you know what restrains him now, so that in his time he will be revealed. For the mystery of lawlessness is already at work; only he who now restrains will do so until he is taken out of the way. Then the lawless one will be revealed whom the Lord will slay with the breath of His mouth and bring to an end by the appearance of His coming; that is, the one whose coming is in accord with the activity of Satan, with all power and signs and false wonders, and with all the deception of the wickedness for those who perish, because they did not receive the love of the truth so as to be saved. For this reason God will send upon them a deluding influence so that they will believe what is false, in order that they all may be judged who did not believe the truth, but took pleasure in wickedness. (2 Thess. 2:1–12, NASB)

PAUL'S REVELATION ABOUT THE MAN OF SIN – F

- What is the timing "concerning the coming of our Lord Jesus Christ" (v.1)?
- Why do some Bibles have "day of Christ" while others the "day of the Lord" (v. 2)?
- When does "the falling away" occur (v. 3)?
- Where does the Antichrist sit while proclaiming to be God (v. 4)?
- What is holding back the Antichrist from surfacing on the world's scene (vv. 6–7)?
- Will Jesus kill the Antichrist when He returns (compare v. 8 and Rev. 19:20)?
- Why do people get banished to the lake of fire (v. 10)?
- What is the "strong delusion" (v. 11)?

PAUL'S REVELATION ABOUT THE MAN OF SIN – I

The Greek opening word order for 2 Thessalonians 2:1 perfectly matches that of 1 Thessalonians 5:12, and could be translated "but we request you, brethren." Closing out the verse in the NKJV are the words, "we ask you." Yet the English translation is as follows: "Now, brethren, concerning the coming of our Lord Jesus Christ and our gathering together to Him, we ask you" (v. 1). The Greek particle translated "now" shows a transition from Paul's prayer (1:11–12) to a new subject. Paul doesn't command these saints, but *inquires* or *asks*, as shown by the entreaty "we ask." He then uses the familiar term "brethren," communicating an intimate friendship with his spiritual children.

One article joins "the coming of our Lord Jesus Christ and our gathering together to Him" referencing the same event. Moreover "our" occurs twice: the first time in relation to the return of Jesus, and again with the gathering accompanied by Him, which expresses the personal interest of the writers and recipients of the letter. "The coming" points to a personal visit by Jesus. The extended stay of the saints with the Lord begins at the Rapture (1 Thess. 4:13–18), which is being addressed here. "Gathering" only occurs twice in the Greek New Testament. Hebrews 10:25 uses the term (translated "assembling together") of the regular fellowship of the saints, foreshadowing the future uninterrupted bliss of being with Jesus and fellow believers when He returns.

"Not to be soon shaken in mind or troubled," continues Paul, "either by spirit or by word or by letter, as if from us, as though the day of Christ had come" (v. 2). The opening Greek structure shows purpose. Paul writes with the intent to allay the misapprehensions of these saints. The adverb "soon" carries the notion of *rashly* or *hastily*, while "shaken" calls attention *to move back and forth*. Its first appearance in the Greek New Testament is Matthew 11:7, describing "a reed shaken by the wind." Also, Luke applies the word to an earthquake: "suddenly there was a great earthquake, so the foundations of the prison were shaken" (Acts 16:26). Paul employs the term metaphorically to be "shaken in mind."

Next, the apostle deploys another verb translated "troubled." Interestingly, "shaken" occurs in the aorist tense, directing us to the beginning of the uneasiness, and "troubled" surfaces as a present tense verb, showing the continual disturbance. Both "shaken" and "troubled" are passive verbs—showing the effects the three agents producing the agitation cause. Furthermore, all three deceptions are introduced with the same preposition translated "by" (meaning "by" or "through"), communicating three separate means.

Prophecy existed in the church at Thessalonica (1 Thess. 5:20), and its misuse is the first means of deception ("either by spirit"). John writes that believers need to evaluate spirits (1 John 4:1–3). A prophetic message comes to this church through a deceptive spirit. They also received a verbally preached message, as indicated "by word." The third line of seduction arrives "by letter." All three modes of fraud "as if from us" claim to be from Paul, Silas, and Timothy.

These saints are led astray to believe "the day of Christ had come." Yet the NASB has the words "the day of the Lord," which would point to the dark period known as the Tribulation (Amos 5:18), and the New Testament carries the day of the Lord into the millennial kingdom (2 Pet. 3:10). Personally, I believe "the day of Christ" is accurate, reflecting the majority of existing Greek manuscripts. The "day of Christ" is the time of blessing for the church beginning with the Rapture and expresses the joy of the church-age saint throughout the Tribulation with Jesus in heaven and then the Millennium.

Paul imparts all seven New Testament uses of this special period (1 Cor. 1:8; 5:5; 2 Cor. 1:14; Phil. 1:6; 1:10; 2:16; 2 Thess. 2:2). Sadly, the three deceitful communications had the Thessalonian saints believing they had missed the Rapture and now were in the Tribulation! Also, if Paul had taught a posttribulational Rapture (that Jesus doesn't return for the church until the end of the Tribulation), then the saints would not be distressed, since they would expect the activities of 2 Thessalonians 2:4. Clearly Paul has taught these saints that Jesus would deliver them before the period of wrath known as the Tribulation (1 Thess. 1:10; 5:9).

Paul allays the concerns of the believers by showing two key events that would happen in the Tribulation that they would be experiencing if they missed the Rapture. "Let no one deceive you by any means; for that Day will not come unless the falling away comes first, and the man of sin is revealed, the son of perdition" (v. 3). *To thoroughly deceive* transmits the meaning of the verb "deceive." It arises five times from the Greek New Testament and appears in 2 Corinthians 11:3 "as the serpent deceived Eve."

179

The "Day" refers to the "day of Christ," and Paul gives two arguments why the saints didn't miss the Rapture. There must first be a "falling away." Significantly, the term does not describe authentic believers departing from the faith, but those who profess to know him without sincere faith who then abandon the Lord. It emerges in the Old Testament (from the Septuagint, LXX) in Joshua 22:22 while describing Israel's rebellion. The only other New Testament occurrence is Acts 21:21, about abandoning the Law of Moses. "Falling away" in the context of 2 Thessalonians 2 is during the Tribulation. If Paul refers to the church-age apostasy as in 1 Timothy 4:1–5 and 2 Timothy 3:1–5, then the saints could believe they were already in the Tribulation, since this apostasy existed and the apostle would negate his own reasoning.

Jesus addresses the topic of apostasy during the Tribulation. He lists several things that will happen during the first part of this period. (Observe that in Matthew 24:8 He calls these things "the beginning of sorrows.") Our Lord says, "Take heed that no one deceives you. For many will come in My name, saying, 'I am the Christ,' and will deceive many" (Matt. 24:4–5). Faithfully God saves 144,000 Jews during the first part of the Tribulation who evangelize the lost (Rev. 7:1–8), then He raises up two witnesses (Rev. 11), and is followed by an angel preaching the gospel (Rev. 14:6). Although many hear and initially identify with Jesus, they will fall away as the deception intensifies (Matt. 24:24).

Second, "the man of sin is revealed." Daniel 9:24–27 gives the account of the Antichrist's activity. He makes a covenant with Israel for seven years; however, he breaks that pledge in the middle of the commitment. This is when he goes into the future temple in Jerusalem and claims to be God (2 Thess. 2:4). (We will further probe his origin and activity under relationship.) Paul adds the detail that "the man of sin" is also "the son of perdition." He can be categorized as a person who will experience perpetual ruin. Judas also receives the same designation (John 17:12). He is a true apostate; Judas sells out

Jesus for thirty pieces of silver (Matt. 27:9) and like the Antichrist would know eternal punishment.

Furthermore, the Antichrist "opposes and exalts himself above all that is called God or that is worshiped, so that he sits as God in the temple of God, showing himself that he is God" (v. 4). The Antichrist does not piggyback on another religion; he claims to be God (Dan. 11:37). Paul gives the result ("so that") of his self-exaltation: "he sits as God in the temple of God." Currently there is not a temple in Jerusalem; however, there will be a future temple (Dan. 9:24–27) and the son of perdition will blaspheme the true God (Dan. 7:25; Rev. 13:1–6).

Paul then asks a question expecting the answer yes. "Do you not remember that when I was still with you I told you these things?" (v. 5). The verb "I told you" is an imperfect tense verb showing continuous action in past time. In other words, Paul says "I kept telling you these things." Had the saints heeded the apostle's words, they would not have been deceived through the unholy triad.

What power is able to hold back the Antichrist from his dastardly practices? "And now you know what is restraining, that he may be revealed in his own time. For the mystery of lawlessness is already at work; only He who now restrains will do so until He is taken out of the way" (vv. 6–7). Many have conjectured over the force "restraining" the Antichrist. The verb "restraining" comes from a compound Greek term; it has a pronoun affixed to it showing intensity and the verb *I have*. It also surfaces in the neuter gender. So, what impersonal force keeps the man of sin from being revealed? Just as the Son of God is revealed in "the fullness of time" (Gal. 4:4), so the emissary from Satan is revealed at the designated time.

Paul shares, "for the mystery of lawlessness is already at work." The term "mystery" refers to a sacred secret unknown in the past but now revealed. There has been a spirit of antichrist for more than two thousand years. "Little children, it is the last hour," writes John, "and as you have heard that the Antichrist is coming, even now many antichrists have come, by which we know it is the last hour" (1 John

2:18). We learn from the New Testament many details previously unknown about the spirit of antichrist operating since the inception of the church and concerning the Antichrist.

The apostle who used the neuter verb in the previous verse for "restraining" now transitions to the masculine verb "restrains." The only power in the universe who could hold back the activity of the Antichrist consists not of human government, but the Holy Spirit. Why then does Paul first use the neuter verb and then the masculine? Since the term "spirit" from the Greek is neuter, Paul uses the neuter in conformity to the language; he applies the masculine to the Holy Spirit when His person is emphasized. For instance, John 16:13 uses both the masculine and neuter referring to the Holy Spirit. "However, when He [the masculine pronoun speaks of His person], the Spirit [the Greek term for "Spirit" is neuter] of truth, has come, He will guide you into all truth."

Therefore the "Restrainer" is none other than the Holy Spirit. Once He is removed through the Rapture (having indwelt believers since the birth of the church), the Holy Spirit will again minister similarly as before the church age.

"And then the lawless one will be revealed, whom the Lord will consume with the breath of His mouth and destroy with the brightness of His coming" (v. 8). Another key indicator revealing the person of the Antichrist is the setting up of the abomination of desolation in the temple (Dan. 9:27; 12:11; Rev. 13:14–15). Jesus says, "Therefore when you see the abomination of desolation, spoken of by Daniel the prophet, standing in the holy place . . . then let those who are in Judea flee to the mountains" (Matt. 24:15–16). This wicked deed will be done in the second half of the Tribulation called "the time of Jacob's trouble" (Jer. 30:7) and the "great tribulation" (Matt. 24:21).

Jesus will "consume" the Antichrist "with the breath of His mouth." The verb "consume" derives from the preposition *up* and the verb *to take*. Paul adds "and destroy with the brightness of His coming." To "destroy" means *to render inoperative, nullify, useless*, and *ineffective*. Abruptly Jesus puts an end to the reign of the Antichrist by snatching him up alive, rendering his person and deeds inoperative, and throwing him while living into the lake of fire. John writes, "Then the beast [antichrist] was captured, and with him the false prophet who worked signs in his presence, by which he deceived those who received the mark of the beast and those who worshiped his image. These two were cast alive into the lake of fire burning with brimstone" (Rev. 19:20).

"The coming of the lawless one is according to the working of Satan, with all power, signs, and lying wonders" (v. 9). Behind the reign of the Antichrist is the devil. John writes, "The dragon [Satan] gave him his power, his throne, and great authority" (Rev. 13:2). Satan imitates the works of Jesus. Observe Peter's description of Jesus, "Men of Israel, hear these words: Jesus of Nazareth, a Man attested by God to you by miracles, wonders, and signs which God did through Him in your midst, as you yourselves also know" (Acts 2:22). As Jesus' service displays His deity by "miracles, wonders, and signs," so Satan imitates "with all power, signs, and lying wonders."

Paul attributes to the Antichrist "all power." In other words, he displays *achieving power*. Next, he shows "signs," which are *miraculous accomplishments with a purpose* (Rev. 13:13–14). The word "lying" in "lying wonders" is used first in the Greek New Testament of Satan (John 8:44). "Wonders" derives from the verb conveying *to keep*. Satan captures the world's attention through his "lying wonders" (Rev. 13).

Paul's description continues, "and with all unrighteous deception among those who perish, because they did not receive the love of the truth, that they might be saved" (v. 10). The Wicked One dupes "those who perish" with "deception." Seven times the noun "deception" appears in the Greek New Testament and means *to deceive, bring into error*, and *deceit*. Matthew first uses the term while writing about the "deceitfulness of riches" (Matt. 13:22). Paul doesn't say that those who are deceived are duped as a result of being elected by God to damnation, but that they perish "because they did not receive the love of the truth that they might be saved." Since they reject the offer of salvation by the One who is "the truth" (John 14:6), then they are excluded forever from His presence.

Paul closes out the paragraph as follows: "And for this reason God will send them strong delusion, that they should believe the lie, that they all may be condemned who did not believe the truth but had pleasure in unrighteousness" (vv. 11–12). "For this reason" points to the rejection of truth. As a result the Lord dispatches a "strong delusion," which literally means *a working of error*. In essence the objective genitive ("delusion") speaks of a working leading to error or delusion. The rejection of God's truth through the 144,000 evangelists (Rev. 7), two witnesses (Rev. 11), and gospel-preaching angel (Rev. 14:6) moved them away from knowing the Lord personally and to embrace satisfaction in those things they ought not to enjoy.

Now that the interpretation phase of our study is complete, let us ponder the extensive implications.

PAUL'S REVELATION ABOUT THE MAN OF SIN – R

The New Testament takes us to a new level of understanding about the Antichrist. Throughout the ages Christians have tried to peg his identity and from whence he arrives. Although the former question cannot be answered, I believe the latter can. Traditionally, the man of sin has been believed to derive from Rome, based upon Daniel 9:24–27. We will first examine the term Antichrist, then consider Daniel 9:24–27, and then consider another passage traditionally assigned to Satan which better describes the Antichrist.

The Greek title "Antichrist" occurs five times in the New Testament. Literally the term means *against Christ* and secondarily *in place of Christ*. John is the only biblical writer to use this expression, although other books of the Bible refer to him, but by other names. John initially used this word twice in 1 John 2:18, "Little children, it is the last hour; and as you have heard that the Antichrist is coming, even now many antichrists have come, by which we know that it is the last hour." The apostle made a distinction between the many purveyors of falsehood of his generation who preach an anti-Christian message and the future Antichrist.

John revealed the unified nature of both the antichrists and the Antichrist. He asks, "Who is a liar but he who denies that Jesus is the Christ? He is antichrist who denies the Father and the Son" (1 John 2:22). He added, "and every spirit that does not confess that Jesus Christ has come in the flesh is not of God. And this is the spirit of the Antichrist, which you have heard was coming, and is now already in the world" (1 John 4:3). The fifth reference states, "For many deceivers have gone out into the world who do not confess Jesus Christ as coming in the flesh. This is a deceiver and an antichrist" (2 John 7).

Let's now transition to the book of Daniel. Two reasons are primarily given for Rome being designated the fourth unnamed kingdom (from whence the Antichrist comes) in Daniel 2 and Daniel 7. The first argument is historical, since the three named kingdoms in Daniel in succession are Babylon, the Medo-Persian Empire, and Greece. Since Rome follows historically, it is traditionally dubbed the fourth kingdom.

The second rationale comes from the prediction in Daniel 9:26: "And the people of the prince who is to come shall destroy the city and the sanctuary." It is generally assumed that the verse is a reference to Rome and the destruction of the Jewish temple in AD 70, which means that the prince who is to come derives from Rome.

There are two primary points of focus in Daniel 9:24–27: the sixty-ninth and seventieth weeks of the prophecy. The term "weeks" is not a good translation and should be "sevens." Since the context of the passage pertains to years (Dan. 9:2), Daniel writes about 483 years and 490 years respectively. We are informed, "Know therefore and understand, that from the going forth of the command to restore and build Jerusalem until Messiah the Prince, there shall be seven weeks and sixty-two weeks" (Dan. 9:25). The prophecy commences in 444 BC with the command of Artaxerxes to rebuild the wall of Jerusalem (Nehemiah 2). Jesus riding into Jerusalem during the Triumphal

Entry (Luke 19:35–42) and presenting Himself as the Messiah in AD 33 fulfills the sixty-ninth prediction of sevens (or 483 years)!

Daniel's seventieth week pertains to the Tribulation (Dan. 9:27). It matches the timeframe of Revelation 6–19, which lasts seven years. The Antichrist's activity during this period is recorded in Daniel 9:27: "Then he shall confirm a covenant with many for one week [seven years]; but in the middle of the week he shall bring an end to the sacrifice and offering. And on the wing of abominations shall be one who makes desolate." As we've previously studied, the Antichrist makes a covenant with Israel for seven years and violates that covenant at the midpoint of the Tribulation by erecting the abomination of desolation in the temple at Jerusalem (Rev. 13).

Clearly the scope of Daniel 9:24–27 consists of two things: Jesus' Triumphal Entry and the activity of the Antichrist during the Tribulation. Now consider Daniel 9:26 in light of the range of the passage. "And after the sixty-two weeks Messiah shall be cut off, but not for Himself; and the people of the prince who is to come shall destroy the city and the sanctuary. The end of it shall be with a flood, and till the end of the war desolations are determined." Messiah dies just days after His Triumphal Entry, which purview is in our passage; however, the reference to "the prince who is to come" does not point to the temple's destruction in AD 70 by the Romans.

The Antichrist is not predicted in Daniel 9:26 to come from Rome because the destruction of the temple in AD 70 is not the range of the passage; therefore, the Antichrist does not come from Rome. Rather, he is described in the same verse as bringing devastation to Jerusalem and the temple during the Tribulation, which remains within the one of two focal points in Daniel 9:24–27, which passage corresponds to Zechariah 14:1–4. Moreover, why does Ezekiel receive specifications for a new temple in Jerusalem for the Millennium (Ezek. 40–48)? It is because the Antichrist destroys the temple during the great tribulation as predicted in Daniel 9:26. Elsewhere the destruction of the temple in AD 70 is predicted (Luke 19:43–44), but it does not fit the context of Daniel 9:24–27.

We've already seen that the Tribulation lasts for seven years and officially begins with the Antichrist making a covenant with Israel for that period of time (Dan. 9:27). However, the same verse reveals that at the midpoint of the Tribulation he will break the covenant and "shall bring an end to sacrifice and offering. And on the wing of abominations shall be one who makes desolate." Revelation 13 further reveals that the man of sin will desecrate the Temple that will be erected in Jerusalem by setting up an idol that comes to life!

He will declare himself to be God in that very same temple. Daniel describes his impudence, "Then the king [the Antichrist] shall do according to his own will: he shall exalt and magnify himself above every god, shall speak blasphemies against the God of gods, and shall prosper till the wrath has been accomplished; for what has been determined shall be done. He shall regard neither the God of his fathers nor the desire of women, nor regard any god; for he shall magnify himself above them all" (Dan. 11:36–37). Although many suggestions have been offered about the Antichrist's lack of "desire of women," I believe the plain reading of the text shows that he will either be a homosexual or just doesn't have any need for a relationship with a woman.

Some commentators suggest that the Antichrist will be Jewish because "he shall regard neither the God of his fathers." Yet the word "God" is plural and most likely should be understood as "gods," since he disregards every former god.

Traditionally the five "I will" statements from Isaiah 14:13–14 have been attributed to Satan. I believe that the passage directs us to the statement of the Antichrist when he sits in the temple at the halfway mark of the Tribulation and proclaims himself as the true God.

Isaiah wrote, "How you are fallen from heaven, O Lucifer, son of the morning! How you are cut down to the ground, You who weakened the nations! For you have said in your heart: 'I will ascend into heaven, I will exalt my throne above the stars of God; I will also sit on the mount of the congregation On the farthest sides of the north; I will ascend above the heights of the clouds, I will be like the Most High'"(Isa. 14:12–14). The name "Lucifer" derives from the Latin

Vulgate, not the original Hebrew, and means *shining one*. This term only occurs once in the Hebrew Old Testament and denotes *bright one*, referring to the king of Babylon (Isaiah 14:4).

Unlike the passage in Ezekiel 28 that clearly connects Satan with that text because he was in the garden of Eden (Ezek. 28:13), Isaiah 14 directs us to the king of Babylon, who could be the Antichrist. (Isaiah 13:1–14:23 is a prophecy of the future judgment of Babylon.) Moreover, the person targeted by Isaiah will have a worldwide impact, much like the Antichrist. After his fall, Isaiah reported about his manhood, "Those who see you will gaze at you, And consider you, saying: 'Is this the man who made the earth tremble, who shook kingdoms, who made the world as a wilderness And destroyed its cities, who did not open the house of his prisoners'" (Isa. 14:16–17). Also, he is described as experiencing decay (Isa. 14:11) and death (Isa. 14:18–20). These reasons seem to connect the king of Babylon to the Antichrist.

Furthermore, the king of Babylon derives from a long line of sinners according to Isaiah 14:21, which speaks about "the iniquity of their fathers." His demise is in conjunction with the Day of the Lord (Isa. 13:6, 9), which consists of the Tribulation throughout the millennial kingdom. The region will never be inhabited again after his downfall (Isa. 13:19–22), which fits the destruction of Babylon described in Revelation 17–18.

In summary, the Antichrist will make and then break his covenant with Israel at the midpoint of the Tribulation. At that time he will declare himself to be the true God from the future temple in Jerusalem (2 Thess. 2:4). This is possibly when he will make the five "I will" statements found in Isaiah 14:13–14.

Since we have completed our study about the Antichrist under relationship, let's press on to apply what we have learned.

PAUL'S REVELATION ABOUT THE MAN OF SIN – E

Why do many Christians get tossed to and fro concerning their system of beliefs? It is because they have forgotten the clear teachings of Scripture and have bowed to the doctrine of demons. Paul asks a shaken congregation, "Do you not remember that when I was still with you I told you these things?" (v. 5). Sadly, instead of clinging to what they had been taught by the apostle, they accepted counterfeit doctrine. *Embrace biblical eschatology for a steadfast faith* (vv. 1–5) is our first employment point. Clinging to the truth of Scripture will keep you from faltering as you live in a world system promoting destructive teachings from the pits of hell. Purpose to sit under sound doctrine by godly men and not to ever compromise the perfect standard of the Bible.

The Antichrist's reign is restrained by the Holy Spirit (vv. 6–7) is employment point number two. Only the presence of the third member of the Trinity could preclude the Antichrist from emerging on the world scene to bring his destructive practices. Let's make every effort to not grieve the Spirit (Eph. 4:30–32), be filled with the Spirit (Eph. 5:18–21), and not quench the Spirit (1 Thess. 5:19–20). Living in obedience to the Word of God will permit the Holy Spirit His rightful role in our lives to govern and guide us. Let's commit to allow the Holy Spirit to reach a lost world around us through our godly living!

Thankfully we will not enter the period known as the Tribulation (1 Thess. 1:10; 5:9; Rev. 3:10). Perhaps we will be the generation that experiences the blessed hope of Jesus' return to take us to heaven, enjoy His presence throughout the Tribulation, and return with Him at His Second Coming (Rev. 19:14). *Jesus' Second Coming will end the Antichrist's rule* (vv. 8–12) is our third employment point. Take a moment right now thanking the Lord for giving you a much greater understanding of the end times from studying the delightful books of 1 and 2 Thessalonians!

CHAPTER EIGHTEEN

HOLDING ON TO THE THINGS THAT MATTER

2 Thessalonians 2:13–17

The holiday weekend had just begun and the gas station had long lines. Finally, a minister who had waited twenty minutes to fill his car went to pay the attendant for the gasoline.

"Sorry for the delay," the attendant apologized. "It seems as if everyone waits until the last minute to get ready for the trip he has planned."

The pastor smiled, "I know what you mean," he said, "I have the same problem in my business."

Thankfully, Paul knows the Thessalonian saints are different. They have prepared well for their departure. Yet the apostle has to tweak their travel plans.

But we are bound to give thanks to God always for you, brethren beloved by the Lord, because God from the beginning chose you for salvation through sanctification by the Spirit and belief in the truth, to which He called you by our gospel, for the obtaining of the glory of our Lord Jesus Christ. Therefore, brethren, stand fast and hold the traditions which you were taught, whether by word or our epistle.

Now may our Lord Jesus Christ Himself, and our God and Father, who has loved us and given us everlasting consolation and good hope by grace, comfort your hearts and establish you in every good word and work. (2 Thess. 2:13–17)

But we ought always to thank God for you, brothers and sisters loved by the Lord, because God chose you as first fruits to be saved through the sanctifying work of the Spirit and through belief in the truth. He called you to this through our gospel, that you might share in the glory of our Lord Jesus Christ.

So then, brothers and sisters, stand firm and hold fast to the teachings we passed on to you, whether by word of mouth or by letter.

May our Lord Jesus Christ himself and God our Father, who loved us and by his grace gave us eternal encouragement and good hope, encourage your hearts and strengthen you in every good deed and work. (2 Thess. 2:13–17, NIV)

OBLIGATION TO THE ELECT AND THE ELECT'S OBLIGATION – F

- Why are saints "bound to give thanks to God" (v. 13)?
- What is the meaning of "from the beginning" (v. 13)?
- What does it mean that "He called you" (v. 14)?
- What is the outcome of your calling (v. 14)?
- Can you identify the two commands (v. 15)?
- Why is "Jesus Christ" placed before "God and Father" (v. 16)?
- What is the significance of "loved" and "given" being singular (v. 17)?

OBLIGATION TO THE ELECT AND THE ELECT'S OBLIGATION – I

Paul begins the paragraph with the adversative "but," which shows a contrast to those "who did not believe the truth" (v. 12). "But we are bound to give thanks to God always for you, brethren beloved by the Lord," writes Paul, "because God from the beginning chose you for salvation through sanctification by the Spirit and belief in the truth" (v. 13). "We" receives the emphatic placement at the beginning of the Greek verse. Strongly Paul, Silas, and Timothy "are bound to give thanks." Strategically Paul reverses the word order from 2 Thessalonians 1:3 "to give thanks we are bound," where "to thank" God is stressed, whereas the continued obligation ("we are bound") shown by the present tense verb to thank God is emphasized (v. 13). "Always" expresses that these saints modeled Christ well and regularly (1 Thess. 1:3, 7), and "brethren" adds a touch of warmth and pastoral affection.

These brothers and sisters in Christ are "beloved by the Lord." The perfect tense verb "beloved" shows that Jesus loved them in the past and continues presently. In 1 Thessalonians 1:4 Paul writes, "knowing, beloved brethren, your election by God," and our text states "beloved by the Lord." The apostle gives equal weight to the eternal love of the Father and the Son to these believers.

Next, the apostle gives the reason for the thanksgiving, as shown by the word "because," and adds, "God from the beginning chose you for salvation." The Father's election of His saints is before time, which is indicated by "from the beginning." Elsewhere Paul teaches that God chooses saints "before the foundation of the world" (Eph. 1:4). Also, in 2 Timothy 1:9 Paul pens, "who has saved us and called us with a holy calling, not according to our works, but according to His own purpose and grace which was given to us in Christ Jesus before time began."

Furthermore God "chose" the saints for Himself and His own purpose (as shown by the middle voice verb) "for salvation." A sharp contrast exists with "those who perish, because they did not receive the love of the truth, that they might be saved" (v. 10). The apostle continues by showing that "sanctification" is brought about by "the Spirit" who is daily conforming the elect into the image of Christ "and belief in the truth." No article appears before "truth" in the Greek pointing to the quality of truth, which is the opposite of those "who did not believe the truth" (v. 12).

Paul gathers up the entire concept expressed about the work of God in the believer's life from 2 Thessalonians 2:13, by the words translated "to which." Paul states, "to which He called you by our gospel, for the obtaining of the glory of our Lord Jesus Christ" (v. 14). Although the elect are called from eternity past, we are born again through belief in the gospel (Titus 1:2–3). Our calling leading to conversion is "for the obtaining of the glory of our Lord Jesus Christ." Here the noun translated "obtaining" carries the notion of *acquiring, obtaining,* or *purchasing.* A parallel idea comes from Paul in 1 Thessalonians 5:9, "for God did not appoint us to wrath, but to obtain salvation through our Lord Jesus Christ."

"Therefore, brethren, stand fast and hold the traditions which you were taught, whether by word or our epistle" (v. 15). The Greek sentence begins with two inferential conjunctions, which means drawing a conclusion from previous information. Paul's use of the second inferential conjunction adds strength to the conclusion. *Those from the same womb,* which is the meaning of "brethren," are given two commands: "stand fast and hold the traditions."

The former verb has one literal New Testament use. It appears in Mark 11:25 of someone standing. Every other use is figurative, conveying *to stand unyielding.* It occurs in 1 Thessalonians 3:8 to "stand fast in the Lord," and 1 Corinthians 16:13 to "stand fast in the faith." *To grip tightly or firmly* gives the meaning of the latter verb translated "hold." Both verbs appear in the present tense, so the idea is *to continually stand unyielding* and *continue holding* "the traditions." The saints are not to hold the "tradition of the elders" (Mark 7:3–9) but the Word of God, whether spoken or written, as indicated "by word or our epistle."

Prayer closes out our paragraph. Paul offers, "Now may our Lord Jesus Christ Himself, and our God and Father, who has loved us and given us everlasting consolation and good hope by grace, comfort your hearts and establish you in every good word and work" (vv. 16–17). In unusual form the apostle places "Jesus Christ" before "God and Father" (Gal. 1:1; 2 Cor. 13:14). With an oblique reference Paul again represents the Son's equality with the Father. Moreover, he uses two singular verbs ("loved" and "given"), displaying two members of the Trinity (Son and Father) as one God. Jesus communicates the same truth as follows: "I and My Father are one" (John 10:30).

Two wonderful blessings flow from the Son and Father's love and giving nature: "everlasting consolation and good hope by grace." Since the Lord is eternal, there is no lack of the comfort and beneficial hope He provides. Paul's wish comes through the use of two optatives, "comfort" and "establish." Interestingly, both verbs surface as singular in number, which again points to the Son and Father's eternal essence. Simply put, Paul prays to the Son and Father to comfort (or encourage) and stabilize the saints at Thessalonica "in every good word and work." He desires them to thrive by their useful and beneficial speech and deeds.

Now that we have completed the interpretation of the passage, let's proceed to the relationship facet of our study.

OBLIGATION TO THE ELECT AND THE ELECT'S OBLIGATION – R

How often do you give thanks for the saints? Paul felt compelled to do so for the Thessalonians (2 Thess. 1:3; 2:13). Out of the thirty-nine New Testament uses of the verb, Paul employs it most often. He first applies the term to the Roman believers: "First, I thank my God through Jesus Christ for you all, that your faith is spoken of throughout the whole world" (Rom. 1:8). In the same epistle he lauds Priscilla and Aquila, "who risked their own necks for my life, to whom not only I give thanks, but also all the churches of the Gentiles" (Rom. 16:4).

Even though the saints at Corinth needed much correction from the apostle, he pens, "I thank my God always concerning you for the grace of God which was given to you by Christ Jesus" (1 Cor. 1:4). Sadly, the Galatian church suffers infiltration by Judaizers who want to add the Law to the gospel of grace. Paul does not offer thanksgiving for them and harshly confronts their deviation from the message of the gospel alone to save.

Paul delights in the churches at Ephesus, Philippi, and Colossae. He writes to the saints at Ephesus, "Therefore I also, after I heard of your faith in the Lord Jesus and your love for all the saints, do not cease to give thanks for you, making mention of you in my prayers" (Eph. 1:15–16). "I thank my God upon every remembrance of you" cheerfully writes the apostle Paul to the saints at Philippi (Phil. 1:3). Likewise he shares with the believers at Colossae, "We give thanks to the God and Father of our Lord Jesus Christ, praying always for you, since we heard of your faith in Christ Jesus and your love for all the saints" (Col. 1:3–4).

Yet Paul reserves his greatest accolades for the precious saints at Thessalonica. He not only instructs them "in everything give thanks" (1 Thess. 5:18), but also offers the same for them (1 Thess. 1:2; 2:13; 2 Thess. 1:3; 2:13). The Word of God through the apostle Paul exhorts us to regularly offer the sacrifice of praise to our God, thanking Him for the saints in our lives. Let's follow Paul's lead.

Yes, it is time now to employ what we have learned. Let's do so with great determination to be both a hearer and doer of the Word.

OBLIGATION TO THE ELECT AND THE ELECT'S OBLIGATION – E

Give thanks for the elect whom God will glorify (vv. 13–14) is the first of three employment points. The Lord's glorious work of salvation will be completed. Paul writes, "being confident of this very thing, that He who has begun a good work in you will complete it until the day of Jesus Christ" (Phil. 1:6). Many years ago I learned the acronym A.C.T.S. for a pattern of prayer. The "A" stands for *adoration*; we should begin our prayers adoring the Lord. Next, the "C" represents *confession*; the saints are to faithfully confess any known sin (1 John 1:9). Then comes the "T," which communicates *thanksgiving*. From our study, let's make sure we thank God for the believers in our lives as a regular practice; Paul did! Finally, the "S" stands for *supplication.* That is the aspect of prayer where we ask God for our needs and other things on our heart.

After Paul's giving of thanks for the saints for their election and subsequent glorification, he moved to the believers remaining loyal to God and the Bible. *Stand firm and cling to Scripture as His elect* (v. 15) is our second employment point. Saints have obligations to God based upon their election. We are to be immovable in the faith. Your assignment is to memorize the following: "Watch, stand fast in the faith, be brave, be strong" (1 Cor. 16:13). Strength is drawn from contemplating the Word of God; therefore, we must hide it in our hearts and tenaciously hold on to its teachings.

Our third and final employment point derives from 2 Thessalonians 2:16–17: *Pray for the elect's comfort and stability in word and deed.* The saints at Thessalonica received persecution. Firsthand they needed to experience the comforting hand of the Lord through other believers, and for steadfastness in word and deed. Enduring the attacks of the unjust aligns with the calling of those who know the Lord (Phil. 1:29). Indeed, we not only suffer for the Lord, but also need to consistently live for Jesus expressed by what we say and do. Let's represent Him well!

PART TWO

CLOSING EXHORTATIONS TO THE SAINTS

2 Thessalonians 3

CHAPTER NINETEEN

SEEKING PRAYER
SUPPORT, KNOWING GOD
IS WORKING

2 Thessalonians 3:1–5

Edward McKendree Bounds (August 15, 1835 – August 24, 1913), better known as E. M. Bounds, was an American author, attorney, and clergy member. His books on prayer are renowned in Christian circles. The following quote from this prolific writer should cause pastors to bend the knee more often: "Every preacher who does not make prayer a mighty factor in his own life and ministry is weak as a factor in God's work and is powerless to protect God's cause in this world."

Not only did Paul make prayer a vital component of his ministry, but he also solicited the supplications of the saints for his outreach.

Finally, brethren, pray for us, that the word of the Lord may run swiftly and be glorified, just as it is with you, and that we may be delivered from unreasonable and wicked men; for not all have faith.

But the Lord is faithful, who will establish you and guard you from the evil one. And we have confidence in the Lord concerning you, both that you do and will do the things we command you.

Now may the Lord direct your hearts into the love of God and into the patience of Christ. (2 Thess. 3:1–5)

Finally, our friends, please pray for us. This will help the message about the Lord to spread quickly, and others will respect it, just as you do. Pray that we may be kept safe from worthless and evil people. After all, not everyone has faith. But the Lord can be trusted to make you strong and protect you from harm. He has made us sure that you are obeying what we taught you and that you will keep on obeying. I pray that the Lord will guide you to be as loving as God and as patient as Christ. (2 Thess. 3:1–5, CEV)

PLEASE PRAY FOR US – F

- What does "finally" imply (v. 1)?
- Why pray, "the word of the Lord may run swiftly" (v. 1)?
- How should the term "faith" be defined (v. 2)?
- What is "the Lord is faithful" (v. 3) contrasted with (v. 2)?
- Where does Paul place his "confidence" (v. 4)?
- Do you pray for the saints like Paul did for the Thessalonians (v. 5)?

PLEASE PRAY FOR US – I

"Finally, brethren, pray for us," writes Paul, "that the word of the Lord may run swiftly and be glorified, just as it is with you" (v. 1). *As for the rest* gives us the meaning of the adjective "finally." Paul has completed his instruction on the end times (1:1–2:12) and now transitions to secondary but important matters. He seeks those *from the same womb,* which is the meaning of "brethren," to "pray for us." The imperative "pray" appears in the emphatic position from the Greek and gives a command. Could the apostle's greatness be derived not only from the fact that he faithfully prayed for the saints (2 Thess. 1:11; Col. 1:3) but that he secured their prayer support (1 Thess. 5:25; Col. 4:2–4)?

"That" introduces the purpose of Paul's imperative "pray for us." He states, "that the word of the Lord may run swiftly and be glorified."

He uses the technical expression "the word of the Lord," denoting an authoritative message from God as used in the Old Testament (Gen. 15:1; Jonah 1:1) and New Testament (1 Thess. 1:8; 4:15). His passion consists of the message of the gospel spreading, as indicated by the word "run." This term is used of literal running (Matt. 27:48) and figuratively as Hebrews 12:1, "let us run with endurance the race that is set before us." Most likely Paul has in mind Psalm 147:15, "He sends out His command to the earth; His word runs very swiftly."

Paul knows that if God's Word has free course and changes lives, then it leads to the glory of the Lord. Both "run" and "be glorified" are present tense verbs. The latter derives from a person having a high opinion of someone or something—as Paul does of the Bible, since he knows its ability to save souls and change lives. To the Galatians Paul expresses this very sentiment: "But they [the churches of Judea] were hearing only, 'He who formerly persecuted us now preaches the faith which he once tried to destroy.' And they glorified God in me" (Gal. 1:23–24). Paul's experience would also be the same as those at Thessalonica (1 Thess. 1:9; 2:13), which is shown by the words "just as it is with you."

Another purpose is given by the apostle concerning the prayers of these saints, "that we may be delivered from unreasonable and wicked men" (v. 2). *To draw* or *drag along the ground* conveys the root idea of "be delivered." Three times this term occurs in 2 Corinthians 1:10 of God rescuing Paul. Observe how he applies the verb in the past, present, and future tenses: "who delivered us from so great a death, and does deliver us; in whom we trust that He will still deliver us."

Paul seeks the prayers of the believers at Thessalonica to deliver him "from unreasonable and wicked men." The combination of the past tense verb (aorist) "delivered" with an article ("the") before "unreasonable and wicked men" points to a definite situation. Paul is writing this epistle from Corinth, so that most likely is the place he is threatened (Acts 18:5, 6, 12–13). "Unreasonable" has the alpha privative affixed to the adjective meaning *not* and the root denoting *place,* giving the concept *having no place.* These "wicked men" *have no place* for Paul "for not all have faith." Like those who reject the gospel (2 Thess. 2:10), the unreasonable and wicked men at Corinth have not placed faith in the good news about Jesus' death, burial, and resurrection.

"But the Lord is faithful, who will establish you and guard you from the evil one" (v. 3). "Faithful" is juxtaposed (placed side by side) to "faith" at the end of 2 Thessalonians 3:2. "But" shows the contrast of those who don't have faith in the faithful Lord. We find the words "God is faithful" in 1 Corinthians 1:9, 1 Corinthians 10:13, and 2 Corinthians 1:18. Yet none of those texts have the verb "is"; the Greek reader would naturally supply it. Yet our passage has the verb "is," emphasizing the existence of the faithfulness of Jesus. Moreover, "faithful" surfaces as the first word in 2 Thessalonians 3:3, showing emphatically the Lord's faithfulness.

Jesus, the ever-trustworthy God, "will establish you and guard you from the evil one." The combination of these two future tense verbs ("will establish" and "will guard") emerges nowhere else from the Greek New Testament. The Lord will help them *to stand*, which is the root meaning of "establish," and will *keep watch over*, which is the meaning of "guard." Faithfully the Lord gives an inner stability ("will establish") and outer protection ("will guard") "from the evil one," that is, Satan (1 John 5:18).

Next Paul writes, "And we have confidence in the Lord concerning you, both that you do and will do the things we command you" (v. 4). The translation "and" gives a transition that builds upon the Lord's faithfulness (v. 3). "Confidence" derives from the root *to be persuaded*. Paul uses the perfect tense, expressing a confidence from the past that continues to the present. Creatively the apostle shows the current obedience of these saints by the present tense verb translated "you do" and then applies the same verb to the future tense. He is persuaded by the saints that continuing practice of what "we command you" will be carried out in the future.

"Now may the Lord direct your hearts into the love of God and into the patience of Christ," pens the spiritual father of these saints.

Paul expresses his wish by the optative use of the verb "direct," which has an intensifier (preposition) affixed to the verb meaning *to direct* or *guide*. Earlier he employed the term in 1 Thessalonians 3:11, communicating his desire to visit these saints. Here the apostle prays to the Lord Jesus to guide "your hearts" in two ways: "into the love of God and into the patience of Christ." (Note the double use of the preposition translated "into.")

The love of God can be understood several ways. It could be a subjective genitive pointing to God's love or an objective genitive showing the saints' love for God. I believe the lesser-used plenary genitive surfaces here directing the believer to the love of God, which motivates him to love. "Patience of Christ" can also be a subjective genitive, teaching Christ's steadfastness or an objective genitive demonstrating steadfastness for Christ. Once again I believe Paul uses the plenary genitive, expressing the believer being guided toward steadfastness of Christ, which motivates him to steadfastness.

Now that we've studied our text, let's see the broader implications of the inexhaustible Word of God.

PLEASE PRAY FOR US – R

A needy apostle knows the importance of having the saints praying for his ministry to be successful. He longs for "the word of the Lord" to impact many lives. As pointed out previously, this expression is a technical one in both the Old and New Testaments. Twelve times from the Greek "the word of the Lord" manifests itself (Acts 8:25; 13:44, 48, 49; 15:35, 36; 16:32; 19:10, 20; 1 Thess. 1:8; 4:15; 2 Thess. 3:1). Simply stated, Paul commands the saints to pray for the Lord's blessing upon his preaching for the Word to run freely and vastly.

Paul often suffered imprisonment and chains. He writes, "for which I suffer troubles as an evildoer, even to the point of chains; but the word of God is not chained" (2 Tim. 2:9). Although the apostle knew physical bondage, he had an abiding conviction that God's Word would traverse many paths and touch many lives.

He had personally experienced the power of the living Word; the writer of Hebrews concurs, "For the word of God is living and powerful, and sharper than any two-edged sword, piercing even to the division of soul and spirit, and of joints and marrow, and is a discerner of the thoughts and intentions of the heart" (Heb. 4:12). No wonder Paul often risked his life propagating the gospel of Jesus Christ.

Similarly we can have confidence in the power of the Holy Scriptures. Isaiah eloquently pens, "So shall My word be that goes forth from My mouth; It shall not return to Me void, But it shall accomplish what I please, And it shall prosper in the thing for which I sent it" (Isa. 55:11). I know Paul would approve of us seeking the prayers of others to ask the Lord to reach many souls with this life-changing message.

Are you ready to go to work? It is that time again to apply what we have learned.

Please Pray for Us – E

Seek prayer for the gospel's proliferation and your protection (vv. 1–2) is our first employment point. I would exhort my fellow pastors to build a prayer team as Paul did. Charge those under your care to pray for power in your preaching, and that the Word would reach many both locally and globally. Moreover, if you are not called to the gospel ministry like your pastor, then pray for the Lord's blessing on his preaching and teaching ministry. Whether in the pulpit or the pew, let's pray for the spreading of the Word and God's protection for those being obedient to the heavenly mission.

The work of the ministry involves men and women of faith. Therefore, *trust Jesus to spiritually ground the saints while protecting them from Satan* (v. 3). We must believe that the work that Jesus has started in our fellow believers will be brought to completion (Phil. 1:6). Furthermore, faithfully petition the Almighty to watch over your brothers and sisters in Christ and protect them from Satan. He is on the prowl (1 Pet. 5:8). Let's remain vigilant in prayer.

Our third and final employment point is as follows: *Trust the Lord for the saints' growth, guidance, and steadfastness* (vv. 4–5). Often we are tempted to take the place of God concerning the growth of fellow Christians. Sadly, we can overestimate our importance, believing we are maturing the saints in our own strength. May I encourage you to be faithful to your discipleship ministry, but also to keep in mind that Jesus is the One building His church? God has faithfully planted the Holy Spirit in each believer. He alone has the ability to make us faithful and fruitful, and to guide us. Please take time right now to evaluate your faith in the Lord's ability to finish His mission, and make any necessary attitude adjustments for the glory of God!

CHAPTER TWENTY

CONFRONTING IDLE BUSYBODIES

2 Thessalonians 3:6–18

Two warehouse workers are talking. The woman says, "I can make the boss give me the day off."

Intrigued, the man replies, "And how would you do that?"

She answers, "Just wait and see."

Next, she hangs upside down from the ceiling. Just then the boss comes in and says, "What are you doing?"

The woman replies, "I'm a light bulb."

The boss then says, "You've been working so much that you've gone crazy. I think you need to take the day off."

Suddenly the man starts to follow her, and the boss says, "Where are you going?"

He replies, "I'm going home, too. I can't work in the dark."

Like these weary warehouse workers, some of the Thessalonians are not desirous to work. Paul's first epistle to the believers refers to those not working and are unruly. He pens about the slackers, "that you also aspire to lead a quiet life, to mind your own business, and to work with your own hands, as we commanded you" (1 Thess. 4:11). Then he writes about those out of line, "Now we exhort you, brethren, warn those who are unruly" (1 Thess. 5:14). Paul will establish a connection between those not working and the unruly in 2 Thessalonians 3:6.

Please finish our study strongly by carefully and prayerfully reading the two translations of the Bible, along with the familiarity, interpretation, relationship, and employment sections.

But we command you, brethren, in the name of our Lord Jesus Christ, that you withdraw from every brother who walks disorderly and not according to the tradition which he received from us. For you yourselves know how you ought to follow us, for we were not disorderly among you; nor did we eat anyone's bread free of charge, but worked with labor and toil night and day, that we might not be a burden to any of you, not because we do not have authority, but to make ourselves an example of how you should follow us.

For even when we were with you, we commanded you this: If anyone will not work, neither shall he eat. For we hear that there are some who walk among you in a disorderly manner, not working at all, but are busybodies. Now those who are such we command and exhort through our Lord Jesus Christ that they work in quietness and eat their own bread.

But as for you, brethren, do not grow weary in doing good. And if anyone does not obey our word in this epistle, note that person and do not keep company with him, that he may be ashamed. Yet do not count him as an enemy, but admonish him as a brother.

Now may the Lord of peace Himself give you peace always in every way. The Lord be with you all.

The salutation of Paul with my own hand, which is a sign in every epistle; so I write.

The grace of our Lord Jesus Christ be with you all. Amen. (2 Thess. 3:6–18)

Now we command you, brethren, in the name of our Lord Jesus Christ, that you keep away from every brother who leads an unruly life and not according to the tradition which you received from us. For you yourselves know how you ought to follow our example, because we did not act in an undisciplined manner among you, nor did we eat anyone's bread without paying for it, but with labor and hardship we kept working night and day so that we would not be a burden to any of you; not because we do not have the right to this, but in order to offer ourselves as a model for you, so that you would follow our example. For even when we were with you, we used to give you this order: if anyone is not willing to work, then he is not to eat, either. For we hear that some among you are leading an undisciplined life, doing no work at all, but acting like busybodies. Now such persons we command and exhort in the Lord Jesus Christ to work in quiet fashion and eat their own bread. But as for you, brethren, do not grow weary of doing good.

If anyone does not obey our instruction in this letter, take special note of that person and do not associate with him, so that he will be put to shame. Yet do not regard him as an enemy, but admonish him as a brother.

Now may the Lord of peace Himself continually grant you peace in every circumstance. The Lord be with you all!

I, Paul, write this greeting with my own hand, and this is a distinguishing mark in every letter; this is the way I write. The grace of our Lord Jesus Christ be with you all. (2 Thess. 3:6–18, NASB)

LOAFERS NEED NOT APPLY – F

- Who are the "disorderly" (v. 6)?
- What example did the pastoral team set for the saints (vv. 7–8)?
- How could Paul have extended his "authority" (v. 9)?
- Is Paul referring to the inability to work or unwillingness to do so (v. 10)?
- What "are busybodies" (v. 11)?
- Who is Paul referring to in verse 14?
- How are the saints to show respect to the loafers (v. 15)?
- Who is "the Lord of peace" (v. 16)?

- Why does Paul write with his "own hand" (v. 17)?
- How are we to understand the bookends of "grace" (1:2; 3:18)?

LOAFERS NEED NOT APPLY – I

"But we command you, brethren, in the name of our Lord Jesus Christ, that you withdraw from every brother who walks disorderly and not according to the tradition which he received from us" (v. 6). Our English verse begins with the word "but," giving us a transition and contrast. In 2 Thessalonians 3:1–5 Paul prepared the saints for the correction before us (3:6–15). It is fatherly in nature; he addresses the saints again as "brethren." The apostle uses the present tense "command." He has used this term in the past (1 Thess. 4:11), and will throughout our passage (vv. 10, 12).

His "command" is "in the name of our Lord Jesus Christ." The name represents the person whether it is God the Father in the Old Testament (Ex. 5:23; Lev. 19:12) or God the Son in the New Testament (1 Cor. 5:4; 6:11). With the authority of Jesus, Paul confronts the wayward group of saints within the church in the same way Michael the archangel encounters Satan: "The Lord rebuke you" (Jude 9). Specifically, those living under Jesus' authority are to "withdraw from every brother who walks disorderly." In secular language the term "withdraw" occurs of furling one's sails. The present infinitive shows to continually pull back until change occurred in the errant brother.

Paul's use of "every brother" seems to imply the group was not large. Again the apostle employs a present tense verb ("who walks"), pointing to the wayward brother's habits. The erring brother is called "disorderly," the root of which appears in 1 Thessalonians 5:14 along with two other groups: "the fainthearted" and "the weak." Each sinning brother lived "not according to the tradition which he received from us," pens Paul. "Tradition" points to those things that were handed down from Paul, Silas, and Timothy to the Thessalonians (2:15).

The connecting conjunction "for" presents an explanation from the command given in 2 Thessalonians 3:6 as Paul writes, "For you yourselves know how you ought to follow us, for we were not disorderly among you" (v. 7). "Yourselves" is placed first in the Greek sentence for emphasis expressing the readers' previous knowledge. Paul's Greek term for "knowledge" can refer to a complete and intuitive understanding. Yet these saints comprehend the instruction given to them because they are children of God (1 Thess. 1:4, 5; 2:1).

"Ought" directs the saints to the *obligation* or *necessity* upon them "to follow" their leaders. *Mimic* gives us the meaning of "to follow," but refers to a positive imitation and a continual one, as conveyed by the present infinitive. Paul then applies the conjunction translated "for," displaying an antithesis between himself and those out of step with God's design for individuals to work in order to provide for their needs. Paul, Silas, and Timothy "were not disorderly among you." Secularly, the term "disorderly" was employed of soldiers out of rank. Paul applies the verbal usage here; the adjective surfaces in 1 Thessalonians 5:14 and the adverb in 2 Thessalonians 3:6, 11.

"Nor did we eat anyone's bread free of charge," writes Paul, "but worked with labor and toil night and day, that we might not be a burden to any of you" (v. 8). Paul's terminology doesn't mean that his missionary team never accepted a meal from the Thessalonian saints, but that they worked to provide for their needs. The adversative "but" imparts a strong contrast since the evangelists didn't depend upon the Thessalonians for their sustenance, and the present tense "worked" communicates their faithful work ethic "night and day."

Tiresome exertion is the meaning of "labor"; while "toil," a common term for work (see Eccl. 1:3; 2:11, 18, 19, 20, 21, 22, 24), adds strength to their effort. The latter surfaces three times from the Greek New Testament; each time it follows the word "labor" (2 Cor. 11:27; 1 Thess. 2:9; 2 Thess. 3:8). Paul's purpose for laboring continually is communicated, "that we might not be a burden to any of you." He expresses the same idea in 1 Thessalonians 2:9 about not being a hardship.

Paul chooses not to seek remuneration from the Thessalonian saints. He explains that it is "not because we do not have authority, but to make ourselves an example of how you should follow us" (v. 9). "For there is no authority except from God," writes Paul elsewhere (Rom. 13:1). The authority to be paid for their service derives from Jesus. Masterfully Paul shares the principle from 1 Timothy 5:18, "the laborer is worthy of his wages," which is based upon Luke 10:7 and Deuteronomy 25:4. Observe the frequent use of "authority" (also translated "right") by Paul as he makes the case for ministerial compensation in 1 Corinthians 9:4, 5–6, 12, and 18.

A strong contrast (adversative) is employed by Paul as translated by "but" in "but to make ourselves an example of how you should follow us." Paul places "ourselves" emphatically in the Greek sentence. Not only did Paul, Silas, and Timothy preach the gospel, but they led exemplary lives! "Example" appears sixteen times from the Greek New Testament, and the noun derives from the verb meaning *to strike with repeated blows*, which gives us the concept of *a pattern*. First Thessalonians 1:7 uses this term of the pattern or example set by the Thessalonians. The word "how" would be better translated "that" and speaks of the purpose, "that you should follow us." We considered the term "follow" used here in 2 Thessalonians 3:7.

"For even when we were with you, we commanded you this: If anyone will not work, neither shall he eat" (v. 10). Together the words "for even" build upon the command of 2 Thessalonians 3:6 (to pull back from the disorderly) and the example set for the believers at Thessalonica by the missionaries (vv. 7–9). We learn from Proverbs 16:26, "The person who labors, labors for himself, for his hungry mouth drives him on." Hunger is a great motivator for work. However, Paul isn't making an observation; he gives a command—those who refuse to work should not be provided for by other saints.

The conjunction "for" clues us into what triggers Paul to confront the wayward group. He writes, "For we hear that there are some who walk among you in a disorderly manner, not working at all, but are busybodies" (v. 11). From trusted saints Paul is receiving reports about the activity at Thessalonica. "We hear" is a present tense verb implying regular updates. Paul receives reports from his contacts in

Thessalonica traveling to Corinth (where he is sojourning). Again we see the adverb translated "disorderly manner" (v. 6), referring to those brothers and sisters out of step in the Christian marching formation.

Sadly, these individuals are "not working at all." Traditionally Greeks despised manual labor; this small group has either adopted that mindset or they are somehow motivated to inactivity by the imminent return of Jesus. Perhaps they are arguing for not working so as to use their time more wisely, since the Rapture could occur at any moment. "Busybodies" literally means *working around.* The wordplay carries the idea that they are not busy working but are busy working around—in the affairs of other people. In other words, they are not busy where they should be, but are busy where they ought not to be!

Notice Paul's fatherly appeal; he seeks to restore the aberrant saints. "Now those who are such we command and exhort through our Lord Jesus Christ that they work in quietness and eat their own bread," pens the caring apostle. He addresses the group as "such" and doesn't apply a harsher tone, for instance calling them "loafers." "Command" now occurs for the third time (vv. 6,10) and the present tense verb coupled with the present tense verb "exhort" gives the continual thrust that "through our Lord Jesus that they work in quietness," which points *to a quiet life* and *stillness.* Stated otherwise, they need to be *settled down* and not meddling in the affairs of others. Likewise they are to provide for their own needs as expressed by "eat your own bread."

"But as for you, brethren," gives the contrast with the previous group, "do not grow weary in doing good" (v. 13). Literally the Greek emphatically has "but you" beginning the verse. "Grow weary" derives from the preposition *out of* or is used as an intensifier, and the term meaning *bad.* The idea of *losing one's courage* or *to be cowardly* expresses the meaning of the compound verb. It is translated elsewhere "lose heart" (Luke 18:1) and "let us not grow weary" (Gal. 6:9). Paul employs the *hapax legomenon,* which means used only once, "in doing good." The compound term is understood as either "to do good" or "to live correctly, honestly, rightly." Perhaps the latter interpretation is best.

"And if anyone does not obey our word in this epistle, note that person and do not keep company with him, that he may be ashamed" (v. 14). A first-class condition ("if") assumes Paul's proposition to be true. "Obey" comes from the preposition *under* and the verb *to hear*. Unlike the unsaved who don't obey the gospel (1:8), these saints are to "note that person and do not keep company with him." The imperative "note" surfaces only here imparting the meaning *to sign, mark,* or *note* whereas "keep company" gives the instruction *not to mix together* (1 Cor. 5:9). Paul's purpose, "that he may be ashamed" and return to a right standing with God and the congregation.

"Yet do not count him as an enemy," commands Paul, "but admonish him as a brother" (v. 15). The present imperative "count" means *to lead out*. Here Paul applies the term metaphorically *to lead out in the mind*. An "enemy" directs us to someone who is *hostile, an adversary* (Matt. 5:43–44). The erring brother isn't to be treated with contempt, "but admonish him as a brother." Paul employs the adversative "but" with the present imperative "admonish," which literally translates as *to put into mind*. Mature brothers in Christ are "able to admonish one another" according to Paul (Rom. 15:14). Children of God should welcome being admonished by their spiritual leaders (1 Thess. 5:12) and to "warn those who are unruly" (1 Thess. 5:14), which is the ongoing situation at Thessalonica.

As Paul transitions to the final few verses, he writes, "Now may the Lord of peace Himself give you peace always in every way" (v. 16). This is Paul's fourth prayer in 2 Thessalonians (1:11–12; 2:16–17; 3:5). The expression "Lord of peace" is unusual for Paul who normally uses "God of peace" (Phil. 4:9; 1 Thess. 5:23; Heb. 13:20) and "the God of love and peace" (2 Cor. 13:11). Paul desires the saints to experience what the wicked cannot (Isa. 48:22; 57:21). Not only does the apostle long for Jesus to give the believers peace but for "the Lord to be with you all."

Apparently, a secretary or amanuensis writes down what Paul dictates up to this point in the letter, and then Paul finishes the epistle. "The salutation of Paul with my own hand, which is a sign in every place; so I write," imparts the apostle. This seems to be his normal practice (1 Cor. 16:21; Col. 4:18).

He concludes the letters as he began the letter (1:2), with grace. With Paul's own hand he writes, "The grace of our Lord Jesus Christ be with you all. Amen" (v. 18). Paul desires God's unmerited favor that led to these saints' salvation to continue with them until journey's end.

We have covered a lot of exegetical ground through 1 and 2 Thessalonians. Let's once again contemplate the wider connections of this passage.

LOAFERS NEED NOT APPLY – R

Do you know the peace of God? Those who don't personally have a relationship with Jesus Christ cannot experience His peace. "There is no peace, says the LORD, for the wicked" (Isa. 48:22; 57:21). Paul beautifully describes Jesus by the following words: "For He Himself is our peace" (Eph. 2:14). How can you know God's peace?

Paul articulately writes about the fallen nature of mankind in the book of Romans: "for all have sinned and fall short of the glory of God" (Rom. 3:23). The verb "have sinned" appears in the past tense from the Greek. In essence, when Adam sinned, so did we since he is our representative. Continuing in Romans, Paul pens, "Therefore, just as through one man sin entered the world, and death through sin, and thus death spread to all men, because all sinned" (Rom. 5:12). Our representative failed us, and thus all people experience sin and death.

However, is death all there is? No! Paul explains, "For the wages of sin is death, but the gift of God is eternal life in Christ Jesus our Lord" (Rom. 6:23). As the second part of the verse refers to eternal life, the first part of the text points to eternal death. John calls this "the second death" in Revelation 20:6. The first death is physical, and the second is eternal separation from God.

Mankind would be doomed had it not been for the intervention of God. Paul shares, "But God demonstrates His own love toward us, in that while we were still sinners, Christ died for us" (Rom. 5:8). The apostle refers to substitutionary atonement. That is, Jesus took our place on the cross and experienced the wrath of God for you and me. How then can a sinner be made right with God? Once again, I turn to Paul: "For He made Him who knew no sin to be sin for us, that we might become the righteousness of God in Him" (2 Cor. 5:21). You need to turn to Jesus Christ who is "the way, the truth, and the life," because "no one comes to the Father except through Me" (John 14:6).

As the Thessalonians repented of the sin of unbelief as worshipers of false gods (1 Thess. 1:9), you need to turn to Jesus Christ as the substitute for your sin. Place your faith in His finished work, and you will experience the peace of God. You can then concur with the apostle Paul and the saints at Rome: "Therefore, having been justified by faith, we have peace with God through our Lord Jesus Christ" (Rom. 5:1). Believe in Him today and know His eternal peace!

Wow! We have covered a lot of biblical ground. Let's finish strong with our final employment points.

LOAFERS NEED NOT APPLY – E

Do you personally know any biblical loafers in the church? If so, the first employment point is for you: *Promote work to the saints while laboring diligently yourselves* (vv. 6–15). This two-part application addresses some of the foundational principles of life. God Himself worked six days and then rested the seventh, giving us a pattern for life. For this reason, you need to exhort those able-bodied saints who neglect work to repent. Be kind to them but also firm, as the apostle has exhibited to the saints at Thessalonica.

Also, you need to evaluate your own work ethic. Paul, Silas, and Timothy led exemplary lives and could call upon the saints to imitate their physical and spiritual examples. Your assignment is to first evaluate your own work ethic. If it is lacking, then make the necessary changes. Then you are to go to those within the body of Christ exhorting them to do likewise.

Permit Jesus' peace and grace to rule your life (vv. 16–18) is the second employment point. Paul writes, "Now may the Lord of peace Himself give you peace always in every way" (v. 16). Walking with Jesus produces His peace in your life; note that the third fruit mentioned in the fruit of the Spirit is peace (Gal. 5:22). Maintain your daily devotions through your Bible readings, study, memorization, meditation, and couple it with prayer (Phil. 4:6–7). Those disciplines will promote God's peace to govern your existence.

Finally, allow God's grace to accomplish His will. You began the Christian journey by God's grace (Eph. 2:8–9), and it will strengthen you until you complete God's course for your life (1 Cor. 15:10). Daily go to "the throne of grace" and seek the Lord's favor upon all that He has called you to accomplish (Heb. 4:16). "The grace of our Lord Jesus Christ be with you all. Amen" (2 Thess. 3:18).

CPSIA information can be obtained
at www.ICGtesting.com
Printed in the USA
LVHW022147220920
666821LV00005B/521

9 781632 695499